Dear Mariella...

Dear Mariella...

An Indispensable Guide to Twenty-first-century Living

Mariella Frostrup

BLOOMSBURY

First published in Great Britain 2004
This paperback edition published 2005

Copyright © 2004 by Mariella Frostrup

Illustrations copyright © 2004 by Øyvind Torseter

The moral right of the author has been asserted

A CIP catalogue record for this book
is available from the British Library

Bloomsbury Publishing Plc, 38 Soho Square, London W1D 3HB

Grateful acknowledgement to the *Observer* for permission to reproduce these pieces.

ISBN 0 7475 7708 0
9780747577089

10 9 8 7 6 5 4 3 2 1

All papers used by Bloomsbury Publishing are natural,
recyclable products made from wood grown in well-managed forests.
The manufacturing processes conform to the
environmental regulations of the country of origin.

Typeset by Palimpsest Book Production Limited
Polmont, Stirlingshire

Printed and bound by CPI Group (UK) Ltd, Croydon, CR0 4YY

www.bloomsbury.com/mariellafrostrup

For J.D.M. in whose arms
I found home

Acknowledgements

This book would not have been possible without the inspiration of Allan Jenkins at the *Observer* and the support of my readers who continue to trust me with their deeply personal, poignant and sometimes downright perverse problems. I am grateful to Harriet Capon and Katherine Greenwood for putting my raw materials into shape. Roger Alton, Peter Straus and Liz Calder continue to encourage me in my writing. Finally, grateful thanks to my mother for having the faith in me at an early age to allow me to make my own mistakes and learn from them.

CONTENTS

Introduction

Once upon a time I was just a struggling mortal doing my best to get on in a tough world. Then along came the *Observer*'s magazine editor, Allan Jenkins, with what he felt was an inspired suggestion: 'I think you should write an agony column,' he said. 'You've lived a bit – you could probably hand out some expert advice.'

I was apoplectic. We all know what 'lived a bit' means. Particularly when addressed to a woman over thirty. I didn't need lunch at the Ivy that badly.

'You won't even allow me the dignity of a post-It Girl phase; I'm straight to Clare Rayner. Allan, I'm not even forty yet.' A high note of unwelcome hysteria had crept into my voice.

'It's going to be a twenty-first-century-style column, a chance for you to debate the emotional issues of the day, using letters as mere prompts.'

'So it's really all about me and what I think?'

'Certainly,' says he.

Well, I have to admit at that moment it started to sound really appealing. An opportunity to rant away on a weekly basis in a national newspaper, get paid and voice my opinions. It was almost everything I'd dreamt of.

The first two columns felt like they went extremely well. Then again they were customised to suit. Each of them incorporated various friends' experiences, spiced up with some recollections of my own, and both were subjects close to my heart. The topics that concerned me then were in no particular order: being single, the treatment of women in the media, a general dismissiveness of blondes. I'm not

1

saying I was shallow but I certainly wasn't casting my net very wide. But I was really enjoying myself.

Then the emails started pouring in. People were writing to me for help and guidance about problems I didn't even know existed. I was mortified. What on earth was I supposed to do? A fine mess I'd walked into. There I was, facing a vast ocean seething with human quandaries: no boat, no paddle, and no clue. This was way too much responsibility. I walked around for two days with the print-outs of my readers' mail in a satchel. The weight of worry contained in that sheaf of papers made the bag seem heavier than the contents surely warranted.

I decided that drastic action was required. One night I sat down and actually read the letters. It came as quite a shock to find myself on intimate terms with so many strangers; especially all at the same time. I experienced one of those Damascene moments you usually only encounter on the big screen or in the Bible. A rare occurrence for those two to have something in common, unless Mel Gibson is in the vicinity. But back to me. The horizon cleared, violins played, the clouds parted. It was just short of an epiphany. After years and years of feeling mildly useless (TV presenting will do that to a person) I felt like I had something to offer. Not solutions, not even my advice. I was never delusional enough to think that anything I said would result in my readers getting up and acting upon it. After all, if close friends, lovers and family won't do what you say, even when they've badgered you for your opinion and you've really bullied them in return, only a fantasist would expect total strangers to show obedience.

No. What I had to offer was something else. Something neither Allan nor I had dreamt of, much less imagined, when we set about the column. It seemed that my warts-on-warts lifestyle had bestowed on me a quality that gave people the confidence to write. I was one of them. Flawed. Approachable in my obvious inadequacy. The fact that my own life to date hadn't been an Eden of exemplary living was finally paying off. This came as a great relief. The very qualities that had initially made me feel unfit for the job were proving to be my qualifications. Somehow, my instinctive, untrained responses, coupled with my own (occasionally public) personal experiences, gave people the confidence to engage with me. From my lowly position in the pecking order of perfection I could stand shoulder to shoulder with my correspondents. Not tower, unapproachably, above them.

Almost half my mail began (and still begins) with the sentence: 'I have never written to an agony aunt before.' That appears to be the secret of the column's success. As anyone who has ever put their problems on paper will tell you, once they're committed to that sheet or have been aired in conversation, you're already halfway to a solution. It's as if the mere process of confronting your concerns can provide a sneaky glimpse of an answer. Then all that's needed is someone to help you focus on it. A chat with your best friend won't necessarily alleviate your woes but there's still a lot of wisdom in the proverb, 'A problem shared is a problem halved.' The very act of scrutinising what is making you unhappy, and then giving it form, whether verbal or written, is part of the process of change. It won't pay off your mortgage, or turn your wife into a sexual bobcat or bring back your husband, or reunite you with your sister, or stop your boyfriend from stashing porn under the bed, or cure your loneliness, or make your mother start taking responsibility for her life. It will force you to open your eyes to the possible causes and potential solutions. I may have just written myself out of a job.

I quickly came to realise with some disappointment that I was just a small cog. Not a prescient saint with a gift for problem-solving but someone offering an airing cupboard for the complexities of modern living. A place to hang out your troubles and then scrutinise them from all angles. Soon I lost my fear of responsibility and happily embraced my bit part in this grand project. I came to see my column as just another available avenue for those who thought they'd reached an emotional cul-de-sac. Somewhere to gather together the dilemmas that define twenty-first-century living. In the process I hoped it would also provide a glimpse of who we are and where we are headed in probably the fastest-moving, most confusing century to date. Watching the news and reading your paper regularly may keep you informed of global news but it's in the minutiae of people's lives that you glean a true picture of the world we inhabit.

You might imagine that my weekly postbag would make gloomy reading but it's not the case. If anything it reaffirms my faith in humanity. Despite tabloid articles proclaiming our descent into a *Clockwork Orange*-style society, criminally-minded, ill-educated, violent, isolationist, selfish, and now obsessively consumerist as well, most people's problems are to do with improving their relationships with those they care about, or finding someone to love. New technologies and inventions designed to make us less reliant on our unreliable fellow humans flourish while we continue to crave a shoulder to cry on, a friend to call, another body to cuddle up to and the right person to focus our love on.

When you're feeling lonely, misunderstood, neglected or plain desperate it's hard to imagine the good in the world. I certainly found it a challenge when I arrived, alone, from Ireland at the age of sixteen and set about creating a life for myself in a foreign land. I battled my way through a short-lived marriage followed by two decades of bad affairs, single life, work dilemmas and self-scrutiny in my twenties and thirties. Nor did I emerge with many answers. No amount of qualifications gives you the credentials to solve emotional angst or unravel practical problems. All of us are just trying our best and that goes for the Freudians, the Jungians, the Buddhists and even those pesky Jehovah's Witnesses that continue to make my Saturday mornings a misery.

The one thing we can try to do in our day-to-day dealings with our fellow humans is to listen. It's a lesson that took me a long time to learn. I was born a fixer and a doer. No problem was too intimidating to be simplistically solved by yours truly. I had an inbuilt aversion to grey areas; depression was a thing to be snapped out of. I hope I've learned to be more tolerant. People don't run like machines, no matter how universal our components might be. Our brains operate mysterious, highly individual programs, which, like today's sophisticated computers, are a nightmare to fix and even routine maintenance is a problem. Partly as a result nobody takes one person's advice and actually acts on it verbatim. Thank goodness. Instead, our natural inclination is to cast the people we share our troubles with. If I've got a broken heart the last person I turn to is a pragmatic friend who'll encourage me to dust myself off and get on with it. No siree, what I want is a sympathetic ear from someone who bottom-feeds on others' miseries, for whom no detail is too small to include. Then again, if I'm having work problems I certainly won't turn to the same friend with her wide-eyed optimism and philosophy that love cures all.

So what of my own credentials? Prepare yourselves for disappointment. I didn't go to university, I haven't studied the great psychoanalysts, I've had a brief and very helpful period of analysis and I've certainly had a share of problems. I hesitate to say my share because I suspect I still have a long way to go. I left home far too young and created a new home far too late. From the age of sixteen to forty I speed-walked through my life, spurred relentlessly forward by my terror of going back. I've experienced poverty, betrayal and quite a number of broken hearts (mostly my own). I've also had a really great adventure. In my speeding years I met fascinating people, visited extraordinary places, made wonderful friends, gained and lost many acquaintances. The one thing I've clung on to is my gluttony for the sheer glory of living. It might have been painful and confusing at times but I've always hurled myself at it with enthusiasm.

Very early on I determined not to let other people's lack of imagination define my life. I've been told I couldn't do, wasn't qualified to try, shouldn't even contemplate, attempting most of the jobs I've gone on to do in my life. When Andrew Neil, then editor of the *Sunday Times*, kick-started my journalistic career, there were groans of dismay from all the papers that have subsequently employed me. I was blonde, for Christsakes: what did I know of the world?

Private Eye amongst others had a field day. I kept only the *Eye* clippings because they made me laugh. My position as one of the Booker Prize judges in 2000 caused high hysteria in literati circles. It was apparently a leap of imagination too far by Martin Gough, the one-man missile behind the world's greatest book prize. When I was asked to make a *Panorama* programme about the destructive effects of 'reality TV', testosterone-powered 'sources' spluttered and then exploded, Vesuvius-like, with outrage. My crime was to test myself, push myself to my limits and continue my education. My only claim for credit is that I refuse to be pigeon-holed. I'm a living reminder that with only the barest minimum of raw materials you can be and do most things you set your mind to. Luckily I never harboured any ambitions as a supermodel. That could have proved a tough dream to fulfil!

Prepare for a cliché. All you need to get on in this world is your health, a sense of curiosity and a small handful of people who love and encourage you enough to overcome your insecurities. I have much to thank my mother Joan for. She believed in me, trusted me and kept my reins loose and her door open. She taught me that love was a force for good and I should show it where I could. OK, so I made a few mistakes over the years on that score! She wasn't a churchgoer and against the odds I've inherited her apathy towards religion. At Loreto Convent in Bray, Ireland, the nuns kept me segregated, in my own private purgatory, three feet behind my fellow pupils. They were worried that my 'uncleansed' original sin might infect the other five-year-olds. I don't chant, I'm not a Christian or a Muslim or a Jew. I don't believe in a bearded white man called God, or an afterlife. As far as I'm concerned, this is it, so we've got to make the most of it. Once I'm dead I'll obviously be delighted to be proved wrong. I may well demonstrate my 'flexible' principles by undergoing a last-ditch deathbed conversion, an opportunistic way of ensuring I don't close any doors. In the meantime I'm a pragmatist. The sooner we come to terms with the significance of our brief lives evolution will stand a chance of meaning more than just standing upright.

As for my correspondents and readers, you're proving to be a mixed bag. I've had praise and outrage heaped in my in-tray and all of it made interesting reading. The bad news, or good, depending on how you look at it, is that our problems are fairly universal.

A man from Tasmania whose hatred of women was obvious from his letter is no longer my biggest fan. My comments on the luxury of 'flexible' working hours for 'nanny-state' employees drew a postbag so large it seemed to prove my point that they had plenty of time on their hands. The girl I told not to chuck her perfectly adequate boyfriend wrote to tell me she'd split up with him anyway but she thought my advice had been excellent! Polyamorists across the country sharpened their pencils when I suggested theirs was the worst of both worlds.

I may not have won them all but at least they kept reading. In our times of deepest despair it's important to remember that there's a world full of people all experiencing similar sorrows and complexities. We worry about friends, children and lovers. We are over-stressed and insecure. We feel lost or alone or eager for adventure. Our relationships are compromised by bad sex, no sex, and no money, or in particularly bad cases, a combination of at least two.

This book won't change any of that, but it might just change your perspective. Other people's problems can make delicious vicarious reading; they also have much to tell us about our own lives. If you've ever stopped in your tracks and just thought: Help! then in these pages you will find yourself in good company.

Mariella Frostrup

I Can't Forget His Infidelity

My husband and I have never enjoyed the same music. He's a Mozart man and I prefer Morcheeba. So, for the last three years, he's been making trips to the Salzburg Festival with a male buddy. I discovered last week (I won't go into details) that they've been enjoying more than the classical festival. They've been visiting an upmarket brothel. I thought we'd had a happy marriage and a decent sex life these last ten years. Now I'm questioning everything, I feel desperately insecure and I can't wipe the images of his infidelity from my mind. Is my marriage over?

No, but I'm afraid you are the one who's going to have to do the repair work. First of all you've got to stop taking it personally. Your husband's behaviour has nothing to do with you. It *affects* you but it wasn't prompted, inspired, encouraged or instigated by anything you have or haven't done. At this moment you're probably scrutinising people in bus queues for signs of their incredibly adventurous, athletic sex lives. You'll be remembering all the times you refused to roll over, were too tired for sexual gymnastics or couldn't be bothered to give him a blow-job. Well, stop it. No matter how many sex manuals and sex therapists and self-help books out there try to convince us of the contrary, most of us are doing the same things in bed, most nights, as we have been for centuries. That's when we're not so utterly exhausted that just cuddling up requires a hoovering of energy reserves. You are in the majority if you've ever been less than enthusiastic about your partner's sexual requests; particularly midweek!

Your husband has indulged in a sexual scenario which the vast majority of men and women fantasise about at some time or other. Indeed as fantasies go, the paid-for sex slave rates very low on the imaginative Richter scale. Prostitution is the oldest profession in the book and some people will try to convince you that such longevity breeds acceptability. Not me. The only person that's ever worked for is Tom Jones. As far as I'm concerned the fact that (some) men are still prepared to pay for sex strikes a blow at Darwin's theory of evolution. Sex with a prostitute is just free-market infidelity. Those indulging in paid-for sex don't understand the true cost and aren't counting the price they're exacting from their partner. Not that you can stop your partner fantasising. I'm at it all the time. Just the other day I imagined smashing to pulp the head of the insufferably smug vegan at the food counter in my local health store. Every time I see Dubya on screen I want to reinact the ear-slicing scene in *Reservoir of Dogs*. I'm not saying it's particularly functional but so long as it's only in my head it does no one else any damage. You can't police your partner's thoughts but you can expect a degree of restraint in their actions.

Men rarely see prostitutes because they're not getting decent sex at home. They visit a hooker to feed rather than address their psychological demons. I don't know your husband so I've no idea what his issues are. You, on the other hand, are well placed to observe and should maybe turn your thoughts outwards, away from self-flagellation, and start figuring out what's going on in his mind. The most common contributor is a lack of self-esteem. The mind can get confused. Sometimes it fails to recognise the difference between someone who likes you being nice to you, and someone you've paid to like you being nice to you. It's a mistake that famous people, powerful people and those going through a crisis of self-worth make. They fail to separate the organic responses of their friends from the sycophantic behaviour of subordinates and end up expecting the latter from all and sundry.

Perhaps your partner has been feeling a little redundant of late? Or perhaps he was three years ago when he first embarked on this sexual odyssey? It's such a cliché but most of our undesirable behaviour just boils down to basic insecurity. Behind every despotic dictator lies a boy who wasn't liked at school; which just goes to show that kids aren't as stupid as we think. It's amazing how quickly a one-off misnomer can evolve into a bad habit. Nobody ever imagines, lighting their first cigarette, that in a short time they'll be on sixty a day and hooked. At least your husband's predilection for sex by wallet hasn't escalated to those heights. Possibly he and his pal just see their actions as an example of occasional high-spirited high jinx? Visiting a prostitute doesn't look nearly so glamorous and daring when you're a single saddo whose partner has left you. Perhaps they should consider that eventuality.

The truth is that I'm all for a little experimentation but sexually I think it's better if both partners are involved. In your case at present it's a little one-sided. I suspect that part of the reason for your roaming imagination right now is healthy sexual curiosity. You might even subconsciously envy him the experience. If so, I've heard there's a place called the Ranch just outside Cape Town that might be for you! Apparently it's a country club where you can just have lunch or accept one of the hunky waiters' invitations to join him in a bedroom upstairs; for a fee. I'm sure there will be women out there saying about time too. Or perhaps you'd enjoy the lurid details of your husband's adventure for your own fantasy bank? If so, then make your partner describe it in full. You might find it quite empowering.

If you'd rather remain blissfully unenlightened then focus on all the positives in your marriage; extract a promise that his digressions are in the past and employ self-discipline to stop your mind obsessing on the topic. Finally, insist he accompany you to Glastonbury next year. He obviously likes to have his music served up with a little frisson of excitement. What could be more adrenalin-inducing than waiting for Morcheeba to come on while fighting off a dread-locked hygienically-challenged garlic-munching waif offering a snog for beer money? He'll certainly think twice before misbehaving in future. The winner in all of this is undoubtedly the Salzburg Festival. I fear your husband may have handed them a brilliant new marketing idea.

I Know I Said For Ever, But . . .

We've been married for twelve months but we can't stand the sight of each other any longer. Is there any alternative to divorce?

Excuse me? May I suggest you actually try being married first. I realise that these are fast-moving times and so on but when you make a vow to stay with someone 'till death do us part', twelve measly months isn't exactly a good innings. Perhaps since it was first explained to me, marriage has changed its nature somewhat. I realise that putting up with Mr or Mrs Wrong for the rest of your life is no way to live but how bad can things get over a twelve-month period? What was the point of doing it in the first place?

These days shacking up together is a more than acceptable option. If you're not prepared to take the rough with the smooth then why not just enjoy each relationship for as long as it runs a smooth course. The minute the water gets choppy, grab a dinghy and paddle off. Isn't it just a bit selfish to involve your family and your friends if twenty-four hours later you're going to start wondering if you've made a mistake? That's how long a friend of mine's marriage lasted.

I was reading about plucky Mo Mowlam the other day and was struck by her description of childhood. Judging by her account her father was a pretty unsavoury character, at least when he was drunk. Since he was an alcoholic we have to presume that was a lot of the time. Despite her daughter's begging to the contrary, Mrs Mowlam senior stayed with her husband until his death some twenty years ago. She then proceeded to lead the life she'd been wishing for during his lifetime.

Now I'm no advocate of suffering in any shape or form. Too many women have sacrificed the best years of their lives to bad men, and I'm sure vice versa, though I've yet to hear about it. But as I flicked through my papers the other day I came across a tale that shocked me to the core. GMTV presenter Kate Garroway and her husband have announced that they are parting. The split is the result of her 2.30 a.m. wake-up call on work days. Now, none of us likes to be woken too early in the morning, and frankly I can't think of a worse job, but Ian Rumsey had been married to Kate for the sum total of two years. Even more intriguingly, the couple had apparently split up before. I couldn't help wondering whether they'd actually made it through the wedding ceremony without a quick break-up. What, I ask, is the point? Why bother getting all tied up in the nitty-gritty of entering the institution of marriage if the way a person stirs their coffee, eats chips, or sings while they're driving is going to lead to divorce six months later?

I'm Competing with Her Mobile

My girlfriend seems to be addicted to her mobile phone. Last night we went out for a 'romantic' dinner and she spent the entire meal texting friends. Then the other day I noticed that she has started switching it on the moment she wakes up. I appreciate that as a freelancer she needs to keep in touch but it's starting to really bother me.

You're not the only one. I've got girlfriends who've given up wearing earrings because they get between them and their mobile. I met a guy the other day whose business plan was to sew a pocket into boxer shorts so the phone was handy even when caught short. In the past week alone I've heard total strangers telling of splitting up with partners, describing their medical conditions, or arguing with their parents via GSM. Either I'm invisible or the world has turned totally myopic.

I don't mean to sound like an old fart but there was a time when it was acceptable to return calls days and sometimes even a week later. Nowadays if you haven't replied within the hour people take it as a personal slight or an indication of a lack of commitment to work or play. Messages buzz through day and night, ingenious devices are invented for keeping phones as close to our mouths as possible without us actually swallowing them, and everyone from Hermes to Samsonite are making mobile accessories.

If you haven't got a mobile you're the Catweazle of the modern world. If you have, you quickly become call-obsessed. God forbid the ring tone should carry on for more than a minute before you answer. Everywhere you look people are scrabbling around in pockets and handbags, behind car seats and in shopping bags trying desperately to catch that call. It's enough to get you screaming out, 'They'll call back.' That's not to say phones are always a bad thing. I'm always cheered by reports of people who have been rescued from sinking vessels in the South Sea or mountaintops, thanks to their trusty mobiles. It means there is some benefit in carrying your personal-communication device to the four corners of the earth. A life-saving call to the Cornish coastguard however is a whole different story to a compulsive text addict telling you they've just bought the new REM album. For some people no experience is banal enough not to detail.

'It's good to talk' was the powerfully effective advertising slogan of one major phone company. I'd like to take out an advertisement myself saying 'It's good to shut up'. There seems to be nowhere safe these days from the verbal assault of strangers. On trains and tubes, buses and taxis, the population is busy belting out their innermost secrets 24/7. So what exactly are we saying? Eavesdrop on this epidemic of callers and you'll glean little of worth about the human race. 'Where are you?' is a very popular opener with 'What are you doing?' coming a close second.

We were told that the technological revolution would free us from our desk-bound lives. Instead it's shackled our desks to us even when we're out of the workplace. Nowadays the working day consists for most people of answering a barrage of text, email and phone calls, very few of which are interesting and only a fraction of which are essential. Like drones we spend our time replying to nonsense without the imagination to question the amount of time we're actually wasting. Meanwhile, clever corporations have used the same technology to build a Berlin

Wall of voicemail and websites between themselves and their customers. Attempting to breach it is like throwing jelly at a cliff face. They've understood how to turn technology to their advantage. Isn't it time that the worker bees replied by calling a halt: a National No Answer Day?

As your girlfriend's behaviour illustrates, there's been an unpleasant development in terms of who receives the benefits of our attention. There you are having dinner together while she busies herself keeping in touch with the less important people in her life. It's a metaphor for what's going on in the wider world. New technology provides the medium for avoiding meaningful encounters with anybody. A few years ago when Daniel Day Lewis famously dumped his girlfriend by fax the world was outraged. Nowadays we'd be impressed that he took the time to commit his thoughts to paper. It would have been so much easier just to text her: 'U r dmpd'. It's good to talk but for two minutes, sandwiched between stepping off the tube and into a meeting? In the five minutes while you wait for a take-away coffee? Impatiently in a lay-by, having pulled off the motorway to take the call? In embarrassment on the train, keeping your voice hushed? These aren't conversations, they're communication deflection.

There's only one good thing about the epidemic of phonitis that's going around: the speed with which we've come to rely on mobile phones suggests that we're still pretty adaptable as a species. Wouldn't it be great if we could embrace solar power with the same enthusiasm, or cycling? Your girlfriend sounds like she's got it bad. Unfortunately she's not alone. Voices of dissent like yours are in the minority, but that's no reason not to raise them. I suggest you lay down some rules. No phones at dinner, no phones before breakfast and definitely no phones in bed. Don't count on her complying, though. Who needs a bothersome boyfriend when you can text-flirt for free after midnight? Conditions apply!

No Fireworks in Our Bed

My boyfriend and I get on great but there have never been fireworks in bed, if you see what I mean. Can you have a happy long-term relationship if the sex is underwhelming?

No.

But then again, yes. A girlfriend of mine was having problems with the physical side of her relationship recently and tackled her boyfriend on his lack of ardour. 'You don't understand,' he said. 'With men, desire comes in waves.' I guess we're just supposed to sit around with a surfboard waiting for a big one to come in! Seriously though, lack of sex in itself doesn't seem to be the problem. Some of the greatest love stories in history have either been unconsummated, see Romeo and Juliet or Robbie and Geri, or subject to very long absences, Antony and Cleopatra, Bill and Hillary, Tony and Cherie and even Charles and Camilla.

The course of true love is no German *Autobahn*. It's more akin to a turbulent long-haul flight. There's the excitement of take-off, then you're happily cruising along and suddenly when you least expect it you're out of control and being bounced around the cabin. In between of course are long periods of boredom and sometimes even nausea.

I've yet to hear about a perfect relationship unless you count the one described by newly-wed Joan Collins in recent interviews or the ones described by the couples who feature on *Hello!* covers. And we all know what happens to them! It's virtually guaranteed that if the sex is sublime there'll be another pesky little matter that leaves you less than satisfied. Great sex is also totally subjective. One man's (or woman's) pleasure is another's poison; something I've discovered over the years when occasional bouts of matchmaking between exes and my girlfriends have proved successful.

I once had the nicest boyfriend in the world. The only problem was that he smelt funny. At first I was so excited about having met Mr Right that I dismissed it as an olfactory blip that would work itself out. Three months later if we were in hugging distance I wanted to throw up. It wasn't that he smelt bad, just nauseatingly sweet. It had to end. Yet when I set him up with a friend she confided in me that the minute she got a whiff of him her clothes slid off of their own accord.

It's a sticky business at the best of times. Opinions seem to vary, depending on age, sex, time of the month and the state of the relationship in question. As the experts always say: when sex is good it equals 10 per cent of the relationship, when it's bad it's 90 per cent.

Nevertheless, underwhelming is not a good word, particularly when applied to sex. It conjures up some nasty scenarios. Visions of limp hands, dry kisses, dreary cunnilingus reminiscent of a rabbit nibbling on a carrot, a sweaty body heaving away on top of you with more chance of finding your tonsils than your clitoris. We've all been there and most of us don't want to go back. Yet what exactly is good sex? If someone trussed me up and stuck an orange in my mouth I'd have them arrested but I've got a girlfriend who'd marry him on the spot. One of life's remaining mysteries is who we're attracted to and why. I've got plenty of friends who've had fantastic sexual trysts with people they didn't particularly care for but none that found themselves hopelessly in love with an appalling lover. Nature seems to have her own way of sorting these things out.

If your sex life is on the wane and you take initial physical attraction as a given, then you have to start looking at what's making your sex mediocre.

These days there are a lot of exhausted couples trying to keep romance flickering in the face of an increasingly stressful and insecure lifestyle. One couple I know with children decided to designate Friday nights their own. It may sound boringly predictable but they found that if they didn't make one night sacrosanct they just never got around to going on a date. So once a week they call in the babysitter and set off to the movies or dinner or go for a walk in the park, or on the odd special occasion spend a night in a hotel. They've found that it keeps their friendship and their sex life alive during even their most trying periods.

Then there's the matter of technique. Another friend had a boyfriend whose penchant for a particular sexual practice drove her mad: with irritation! Two years after they first met she finally plucked up the courage to tell him. He looked at her in amusement, asked why she hadn't told him before and the matter was resolved in an instant. You may wonder why she left it so long but in this instance I think she was right. With sex, like everything else, timing is all. In the vulnerable first stages of dating the last thing you want to do is grab a pin and burst the bubble of your partner's sexual confidence.

In these fast-forward times we're all on a warp-factor-five hunt for perfection and if we don't get it instantly we just move on. What's the hurry? While fearful of sounding like Claire Rayner, the most rewarding partnerships are invariably the ones that evolve over time. Whirlwinds have a nasty habit of dying out. That said, if you've tried every position in the *Kama Sutra*, bankrupted yourself on Agent Provocateur, run him baths, soothed his brow and you're still underwhelmed, dump him. Some guys are just plain lazy!

I'm So Angry with My Ex

What do you do when you want to release the anger you feel towards an ex-partner? For just over ten years I was married to a man who seemed the most charming and lovely husband. Then a year after the birth of our child he announced that he didn't love me any more and overnight turned into a completely different person: a bully, an abuser, a drinker, an adulterer and all-round nasty piece of work. The miserable times far exceeded the happy times, so I decided I couldn't allow him to destroy me totally and we separated. As soon as he moved out, he became nicer again, so we embarked on a civilised and amicable separation, which sometimes included sex even though he was cheating on his new girlfriend with me!

I filed for divorce when I met and fell in love with someone else, with whom I'm very happy. During the divorce proceedings he made me feel sorry for him, telling me that he still wanted me and that he wasn't going to stay with this girl, that he was only with her because she was nice and a bit needy with suicidal tendencies. I felt so sorry for him that I gave him a very favourable divorce settlement. You can imagine my surprise when I find out that as soon as he's got the divorce money off me, he's set up home with her and made her pregnant! I feel I can't just sit by and watch this happen. My child and I have been wronged. How can I get rid of this anger that is eating me up? Please don't tell me to let it rest, that karma will sort him out, etc; I don't believe any more that 'baddies' get their comeuppance . . .

So what do you want to do? Reinvent yourself as the Charles Bronson of the dating world? Charge around with heavy weaponry righting the wrongs committed in the name of love? 'Love easy, die hard' could be your motto. You could run yourself up some sort of leather catsuit, become Cupid's own Lara Croft? We could drag Michael Winner out of his string of fine eateries and persuade him to direct the film of your adventures. The lack of moral ambiguity might appeal to him. Hollywood would definitely be keen. Then again if an illustrious career in the movies doesn't appeal and you want to keep your battle on the streets you'll still be kept busy. You may even have to give up the day job to pursue your passion for employing the scales of justice to measure and allocate love and decency to all and sundry. I don't mean to be flippant but you really need to lighten up a bit. You married the wrong man, he turned out to be a bit of a shit and now you're rid of him. Three cheers for the freedom to chuck him out.

Try testing your story out on friends and acquaintances. You'll find that your tale meets with not only friendly, but also surprisingly experienced ears. Yours is a common experience of emotional immaturity and cowardice. Your ex just didn't have what it takes to complete the journey. Experiences like this one are what makes love such a terrifying gamble; it's why people resign from the game, seek therapy and guidance, run away, break down and then in the face of countless failed relationships get up from the gutter, shake off the debris and start again. No one knows what's waiting around the corner, which is why it's so important to make the most of the good times. We're so busy flicking channels these days that we miss the best programmes. The same can certainly be said for our relationships. Everyone else seems to have it worked out, until they announce their divorce. At least you had the guts to measure the positive and the negative and make a strong, informed decision. Even if you continued to use your ex for sex. I believe the sisterhood gives out gold stars for that sort of behaviour. For every destructive relationship there's a better one waiting in the wings. Maybe not next week but certainly in your lifetime. You are perfect proof. Reading your letter it strikes me that you've already had your revenge. You have met someone new with whom you are happy. So why aren't you happy?

I think you're suffering a debilitating dose of wounded pride. It's only because you're not looking at the big picture. Your ex-husband's emotional problems are so obvious that they're embarrassing. He can't bear to have attention shift away from himself. He's proved it three times. It's no coincidence that the birth of your first child, the appearance of your new partner and the moment you opted for divorce all precipitated dramatic changes in his behaviour. The minute you found yourself with an interest other than him he began to behave badly. The moment you turned him out he started trying to woo you back. Can't you see his behaviour for the pathetic attention-seeking it is? You are conjuring him up as some sort of Machiavellian money-grabber with a plan. You give him too much credit. This man can't control his own responses, let alone start trying to manipulate the reactions of those around him. He's bumbling his way from one relationship to the next, buffeted by gusts of his own insecurity. Why on earth would you seek to reap revenge on such a creature? The best form of attack is to turn your back, ignore him and get on with the positive things in your life. I guarantee it will be much more effective than pulling out the big guns.

My Grown-up Brother Still Lives at Home

My younger brother (twenty-eight) has yet to leave home or find a job, despite holding a degree. My mother (who is divorced) funds his day-to-day living expenses, leaving him free to spend his dole on fags and booze. Any time I come home to visit (I'm thirty-two, the middle child), it is as though my brother's energy and motivation have ebbed just a little bit more. (He rarely rises before 3 p.m.) I fear for his future, for his mental and physical well-being, yet feel unable to say anything. I've had some training in psychotherapy, and have strong feelings on intervening in cases where help hasn't been asked for. As well as that, I'm very close to my brother, and don't want to lose our rapport through meddling in his life. On the other hand, I worry that if things deteriorate irrevocably, I will be consumed with guilt for my inaction.

No offence, but your brother is a kipper. Kids In Parents' Pockets Eroding Retirement Savings are the latest rage, apparently. You'll no doubt be horrified to learn that he's not even in a minority. There are seven million of the buggers in this country alone. A new breed of lethargic offspring who just can't summon up the energy or the funds to leave home. Avalanches of articles have appeared attributing the trend to the cost of student loans, high property prices and the tendency to marry late. I'm not convinced.

Why should we imagine that the lethargy displayed by young people when it comes to politics, ecology or their own futures bypasses their ambitions for a life of their own? Once upon a time we couldn't wait to be out the door. Sex, drugs and gulping from the golden cup of independence were all enticing reasons for fleeing the nest. Now teenagers are frequently allowed to do at least one of the former at home, so long as they keep the bedroom door shut and independence is defined by buying your own copy of *Heat* magazine.

What must it be like for the parents? I imagine that the burning desire to have children is exceeded only by the desire to see the back of them once they grow up to become obnoxious adults in their own right. Who wants some sullen twenty-eight-year-old munching cornflakes at the breakfast table? Luckily your mother is spared that sight, since your brother doesn't emerge until after 3 p.m. Perhaps he's embraced this Count Dracula-style life in order to make his presence less obtrusive. He's probably hoping your mum will forget he's there. I suspect she only has to put up with him a couple of hours a day before he sets off to hang out with his fellow kippers, the only people of their generation with money to go out.

Curiously, you don't mention your mother's thoughts on the subject. My concern would be for her rather than your younger sibling, who appears to be enjoying the proverbial life of Riley. She's the one forced to subsidise his lethargy and endure a complete lack of privacy, which in her newfound singledom probably requires quite a sacrifice. Since I don't know what she's thinking, you force me to do some guesswork.

First of all I have to mention the possibility that you are just jealous. There you are, out in the real world, struggling to make ends meet while your sibling has cleverly managed to forgo such stresses and strains for the life of a fifteen-year-old. You could just be sore that you didn't have the foresight to stay put! If your mother doesn't mind and your brother is not complaining, you are the only one with a problem.

It's more likely that having this full-grown baby man about the house is a source of frustration that your mum doesn't want to admit to. We seem to have embraced the American philosophy of child-rearing, which entails your entire world being ruled by precocious little monsters corrupted by their sense of entitlement. These days suggesting you maintain a life of your own is met with gasps of horror from fellow parents. Hanging on to any sort of adult existence is seen in some quarters as pure self-ishness. Judging by the kipper phenomenon it would appear that being held hostage to one's offspring now continues into middle age. The problem being it's their middle-age, not their parents', that I'm referring to.

There's also the possibility that your brother is suffering some kind of clinical depression, which has led to his state of inertia. In which case it's medical help, not my meddling, that he requires. You say you are afraid to impair your 'close' relationship by discussing the topic. How close can you be if you can't discuss something as fundamental as his lifestyle? I'm curious as to why you're afraid to tackle it. Could it be that you and your mother suffer the same handicap – a propensity to avoid conflict at any cost? In which case your brother has learnt to take full advantage of it.

Not being given the full picture puts me at a severe disad-vantage, but the straightforward answer is that if you're not the only one unhappy with the current set-up then it's got to be addressed. Maybe your mother should start by demanding a curfew – say 10 p.m. – and that he tidy his room every Saturday. Or you could try finding him a girl-friend. Once he's got a woman who's prepared to look after him and have sex with him, life with mother will pale by comparison. He'll be off like a shot.

A Voice From My Criminal Past

I have been contacted by an old friend wishing once again to meet up. I've not seen this particular friend for over ten years, mainly due to the fact that he has been, well, detained at Her Majesty's pleasure. Before his incarceration he and I did embark on a series of crimes, mostly insurance and credit-card fraud. I managed to get out of this racket at the right time. However, my friend continued and paid the ultimate price.

I now have a completely different, respectable and happy home life and ironically work as a financial adviser. While wishing to believe that prison brings about rehabilitation, in my mind I am haunted by the fact that perhaps my friend's desire to renew contact is a ruse to lure me back into some of his nefarious schemes.

Should I give him the benefit of the doubt and show him all that can be gained by turning one's back on a life of crime? Please give me your enlightened view on the subject.

Your fellow members of the financial services industry must be groaning in agony as they read your letter. With reputations as damaged as theirs among consumers the last thing they need is someone breaking ranks and admitting to a life of crime, albeit in the past. But first things first. Don't you just hate friends who turn up out of the blue? Who does this guy think he is just marching back into your life again as though you had some history together? Anyone would think he'd been banged up in prison for ten years with time to think about those who matter to him. Ooops, he has.

Seriously, my first question is whose virtue is it you are worried about preserving? Your letter suggests that it's your own 'rehabilitation' that you're unsure of. Otherwise why should it matter if your newly liberated buddy turns up with some hair-brained scheme for making a fast buck? All you have to do is say no.

If as you say you are smugly ensconced in a brand-new life (albeit with startling similarities to your past area of expertise, but more of that anon), then what have you got to fear? Are you worried about finding yourself in an *Oceans 11*-style scenario where your buddy's Clooneyesque powers of persuasion seduce you back into your old trade? In which case yours is a transformation teetering on the brink of disaster. If you are that open to persuasion, having spent the early part of your life relieving people of their money, perhaps following it with a legitimate career in which you're required to do likewise wasn't the wisest of choices? Although I'm not denying you probably have more experience than most of your current colleagues in your field.

Only the other day I had a meeting with a gentleman of your profession who had sold me a pension policy fifteen years ago. He seemed baffled by my fury on discovering that this policy, into which I had diligently been depositing every month since Duran Duran were last popular, was only worth, to the pound, what I'd contributed. 'A lot of people's policies have actually halved,' he said in a vain attempt to convince me that I was one of the lucky ones. Back in the late eighties he'd assured me that the sacrifice of locking away a large part of my salary for decades would seem more than worthwhile when I idled my twilight years away in the Caribbean on the proceeds. I'm not saying he's crooked but I'd be lucky to get a two-week holiday at Club Med for what I've now got put away. I'm digressing, but I so rarely get a chance to talk about me these days.

You should look on the bright side. There's nothing like a friend in need to put your own blessings in perspective. Perhaps all he wants to do is come over, share a couple of pints with you and tell you hair-raising stories about life behind bars. In which case, what could be better? I think it's only human to get a frisson of joy from other people's misfortune (why do you think I've been writing this column for so long?), particularly when you've sailed in the same gale but managed to escape shipwreck. If you're feeling self-satisfied now about your success at going straight just imagine how much better it will feel when he fills you in on how bad things could have been. Denying yourself such a fabulous opportunity for self-aggrandisement would be, well, criminal, actually.

So my advice is to give your friend a chance; after all, you're in a win-win situation. The only road that leads to disaster is one of your own making, where in a moment of weakness you decide to sacrifice everything you have now for some foolhardy get-rich-quick scheme. In your current profession I'm sure you advise on a daily basis idiots (like me) who dream of instant wealth or at least a luxurious retirement. You know better than most that these dreams are as empty as the society that inspires them. Be sure of what you believe and you have nothing to fear. Although if he turns up with a bunch of guys in balaclavas, ignore everything I've said and run!

I'm Afraid to Move On

I have been seeing a wonderful woman for two years, who now wants us to move in together and start a family. The problem is I still live with my ex. We lead almost separate lives and haven't had sex for decades, but every time I think about leaving it sends me into a panic. We have been together twenty-eight years, and both of us have had affairs throughout the relationship. She knows about my girlfriend but wants us to continue living together until she finds someone else. Despite the lack of emotional closeness we are still friends and I feel guilty for all she gave up for me. We met when I was a patient in a mental unit and she was a nurse. She left her job and her husband to be with me and has always felt more like a second mother than an equal partner.

My girlfriend is very different: open and affectionate and loves me as much as I love her. I had given up on finding such passion or closeness with anyone, let alone having a family of my own (I wanted children but my ex hates them and had herself sterilised without telling me), but I feel paralysed by all this responsibility. My inability to make a decision is causing rows with both of them. I wonder if at fifty I am too old to change? Should I stay where I am and accept that nothing is perfect and this is my lot in life? Or am I just too old to be a father?

I've got some bad news for you. I'm afraid it's time to leave home. Most of us go through this agonising separation in our late teens and it's generally made more bearable by the fact that at that point we can't stand our folks. It's more than likely that your experience with mental illness may have delayed your emotional development. Setting up home with the woman in whose care you were placed when at your most vulnerable has the ring of dysfunction to it. Though you're by no means the first: actress Natalie Wood famously ran off with her shrink and look what happened to her.

I think I'd be understating it if I said your partner has 'control issues'. Still feeling guilty about choices she made three decades ago marks you out as a nice guy but perhaps a little over-sensitive? She was a grown woman even then and arguably better equipped at the time to make a responsible decision. If like Ms Wood you'd run off with your psychiatrist there would have been a bit of a fuss. I'm not so sure that shacking up with your nurse is much healthier. It sounds like you have been kept in your place for a long time. Taking a decision on something as dramatic as sterilisation without consulting the man you live with smacks of control and dominance. Anyway, that's in the past.

Why on earth should you wait to embark on a new life because she hasn't nailed hers down yet? The Berlin Wall came down over a decade ago and with it the idea that you could enforce equality. Heaven forbid, she may actually have to be on her own for a bit. It might do her some good. She sounds like she needs to experience the joy of letting go of the strings, the indescribable bliss of not keeping all her balls in the air at the same time. You both have some growing up to do and for that you need to part.

You are lucky in that you are being offered a second chance. Don't let bad behavioural patterns, or worse still, emotional cowardice, steal the opportunity of experiencing a different kind of love from under your nose. You and your long-term partner have wrung the life out of what you once had. Unless you can imagine a totally different future together then take a leap of faith and step out the door. You have both clung on to the sinking ship for far too long, neither of you realising that the boat's long gone and all you're left with is a piece of driftwood and the memory of something more solid. I understand your worry about losing your partner's friendship but if you have been honest and fair then it's up to her. If she's determined to use it as a ransom demand then you must just walk away.

At fifty you're still young enough to be having a mid-life crisis and only too old to develop a hard-drug habit. Becoming any sort of junkie post your twenties is just downright embarrassing. On every other avenue all that awaits you is a wide-open road to the future. Stop dithering, for heaven's sake. Anyone would think you had nine lives, not just this one. Whether you can or can't have children really isn't the issue here, although I wish you the best. Surely the most important thing is that you stop behaving like one? You must grab this chance you've been given and explore the possibilities. Otherwise you will for ever regret this emotional lethargy that you have succumbed to.

Maybe you are a religious man and believe your second chance comes in the next life. It's a dangerous bet to make and I personally don't fancy your odds. You've been playing Hamlet for too long now; it's time to pack your bags and escape the unhealthy environment in the State of Denmark.

My Son's African Bride

My twenty-year-old son is on a gap year in Nigeria. He has fallen in love with a local girl who is older than him and has asked to come back to the UK with him (within weeks of meeting him)! She is from a deeply conservative Christian community. She also has to support and care for her family. They are now insisting that she gets married rather than just moves in with him. Only my innocent son was surprised by this. He has decided to bring her back with him and marry her at home.

Meanwhile my ex-wife has been working against all my efforts by encouraging and supporting our son in his plans, to the extent of offering to finance his fiancée's trip, despite her frequent cries of 'poverty'. So you can guess which parent is now in my son's favour!

I am shocked by my son's stubborn insistence on bringing this woman back to the UK with him. It's obvious she is just using him to escape from Africa. I feel like I am bashing my head against a brick wall in trying to make him see sense.

It's a brick wall that you have built, so if you want to keep smashing your head on it go right ahead. Otherwise I suggest you examine the similarities between your and your offspring's behaviour and sit down and have a good laugh. He's definitely his father's son. It sounds like two bulls have been unleashed in one very small china shop and are charging about without regard for those around them.

Just for starters, I suggest you stop assuming that all Nigerians want to escape from their country. The notion that life as the wife of your student son in a cold unfriendly

city would somehow be preferable to having a respectable job and staying close to her family in Africa is nothing short of old-Colonial snobbishness. You should count yourself lucky that she doesn't want to keep your boy there. If you keep escalating the conflict, his next move might be something that catastrophic – for you.

What would certainly have been a testing time for all concerned has become all-out civil war. It's time you took a step back and surveyed the battlefield. At twenty your son is unlikely to be listening to his elders. After all, in his eyes you probably made your own mistakes when it came to your relationship with his mother. There's no point in getting all prickly about it: that's the way teenagers see it. To them, unless their adviser's record is spotless, it's the equivalent of listening to Elizabeth Taylor giving advice on a long happy marriage, or Vanessa Feltz on the benefits of aerobic exercise. Youngsters have no interest in hindsight. To them, everyone over thirty is an out-of-date fuddy-duddy who doesn't understand the modern world. That's why we're all so shocked when we reach middle-age and discover that we've still got a pulse. I'm not sure I know of anyone over sixteen who can be talked around by anything short of blackmail. Even then, unless you're withholding a Bill Gates-style inheritance, you're unlikely to make an impact.

I do understand it's very hard to sit back and watch your son walk into a premature marriage that frankly has little chance of survival. Particularly in the dog-eat-dog world that they intend inhabiting. University campuses are rife with devotees of la dolce vita, and your boy may well come to resent his constricted circumstances. More optimistically of course his domestic situation might encourage him to knuckle down and do some work instead of chasing skirt. Ironically their marriage would have a better chance of success in Nigeria where the conservative values you mention would encourage them to stay together rather than part. There's also a miniscule chance that he and his girlfriend are one of those lucky couples who get to cut out the twenty years of dating auditions.

Your main problem is that you want to make your son see things as you do. It's not going to happen. It's time to let go of those strings and let him learn to operate alone. If you're smart, you'll leave your door ajar when he messes up. As for your ex-wife, there's no need to lock horns with her. Be generous – every son loves his mum.

If you're lucky he and his fiancée will be happy together; if not, they'll get divorced. Your main concern now should be to ensure that your relationship, the only one you can be responsible for, will remain intact. Your son is as stubborn as you, and you know how stubborn that is!

She Kept Things From Me

I am thirty-six and work in the arts. I have been living with my American girlfriend for six months, which was hard at first as she got a divorce a year ago. But things have been great for the last four months. Before we started seeing one another she told me she was a receptionist in a massage parlour in America, but recently I have found out she was actually a masseuse there, which is where she met her ex-husband (a client) and then moved to England to marry him. This is also why their marriage did not work. I believe she has not told me about her past after the effect it had on her last relationship. I was about to give up work and set up a business with my girlfriend (import–export) when this can of worms landed in my lap. I now feel emotionally confused and that I have been lied to. I don't know if I should mention that I know of her past or not. Do I still set up in business with someone who hides the facts?

I can't help feeling you are comparing eggs with broccoli. Neglecting to tell you the whole truth about her past profession hardly marks your girlfriend down as a crook. Instead I suspect she's wise to the fact that most men won't say no to a lap dance but they won't be taking the object of their interest for a surf 'n turf supper afterwards. It's all very well to employ hookers, strippers, and masseuses for your personal pleasure but you'd have to be pretty desperate to actually wind up with one. Or so the theory goes. You don't have to be a brain surgeon to spot the double standard and I'm sure your girlfriend didn't need to be ditched a second time in order to learn that it probably wasn't a profession it was wise to boast about. Nevertheless I think you're jumping to conclusions when you say the reason her marriage didn't work was because she used to be a masseuse. That said, it's a nice tidy way of making sense of things on your terms and boxing up that part of her past life. No wonder you're happy to endorse it.

It's a natural human impulse to project our own personal understanding of a given situation on to other people's lives. Whether it's suicide or divorce, murder or unfaithfulness, our only means of translating the actions of others is through our own experience. Yet this is also how we make our stupidest mistakes. The human psyche is highly complex and individually unique. There aren't two people in this world of many billions whose emotional responses or processes of rationalisation are the same. It's the reason that seriously listening to those we care about or have dealings with is very important. The most common mistake is to think we already know what someone is saying, instead of actually listening to what they are trying to tell us.

In this instance I gather from your letter that you haven't even discussed this matter with your girlfriend yet. Doesn't this confirm that she's not the only one guilty of bad communication skills? Don't you think a bit of a heart-to-heart might be in order? My guess is that she's unnecessarily embarrassed about her past job and it would be a relief to know it was out in the open and no longer an issue. She's probably worried that you will judge her harshly. I certainly hope that's not the case. We all tell white lies in our efforts to shine in the eyes of those we love. I'm sure if you'd suffered terribly from piles as a child it wouldn't be the first subject you'd bring up on a date.

And why shouldn't we be allowed our secrets? This share-all, get-it-off-your-chest, confessional society we live in is getting a little out of hand. We're increasingly addicted to unburdening ourselves on virtual strangers and prattling on ad nauseam about our inner feelings. Most of the time we're just exercising our lips and end up saying little of value.

I respect your girlfriend's right to keep some things to herself. So should you. Six months together is no time at all. In the best relationships people are still being surprised by their partners after fifty years of cohabitation. Needless to say, one hopes that the majority of these 'surprises' are of a pleasant variety. Not, 'Darling, I'm gay,' after ten years as man and wife. Seriously, I'm all for honesty in a relationship but there has to be a limit. Every human being has the right to an inner life they can call their own without others perpetually peering and prying at it.

Since this knowledge wasn't gleaned from your girlfriend it must have been proffered by some well-meaning 'deep throat'. Their motive for enlightening you on this detail of your girlfriend's past may well warrant more scrutiny than your girlfriend's decision to cover it up. Occasions when friends and acquaintances unburden themselves of delicate information selflessly on our behalf are few and far between. There's nearly always an agenda and I'd love to know theirs.

Finally, don't think I'm being insensitive. I know you're probably plagued by imaginative visions of what her past work entailed. It's not the easiest thing to come to terms with, but try to imagine how much worse it must be for the woman you love. My advice is to sit down, have a talk and take it from there. As for setting up a business, make sure you're doing it for the right reasons, There's a nasty whiff of blame in your statement that you were 'about to give up work'. That has to be your choice, no one else's. I don't want you writing back to me in six months' time saying you gave up your career for love and now you've lost both.

Must She Sleep with
Her Boyfriend at Home?

Although she has no money and only a part-time job, my daughter – who is seventeen – wants to move out and live with friends. I would offer to support her financially but I can't afford it. I've tried to persuade her to stay, and she's said that she will if I let her boyfriend stay over occasionally – and sleep in her room. I think they probably are having sex (they've been together over a year) but I don't feel comfortable with it happening in my house. Am I being unreasonable?

Am I hearing you correctly? Your daughter has been dating a boy for a year, has undoubtedly had sex with him and you don't even know? Here she is going through one of the defining moments of her life, and you haven't even discussed it with her? You suspect that they're having sex? Don't you think you should be in possession of that information? Wouldn't it make sense to have a conversation with her about how it's working out, what precautions she's taking, whether she finds it enjoyable, whether you can be of any help, and how she should deal with her sexuality now that she's embarked on exploring it?

Perhaps you feel that by discussing sex you are condoning it, or that by explaining sexual behaviour you'd be encouraging your children to get out there and do it. I've never understood the connection between awareness and activity. I'm aware that some people get great pleasure from stuffing oranges in their mouths, and then hanging themselves from light fittings in order to achieve heightened orgasms. Does it make me want to do it? Nope! When my mother explained how babies were made, how people in love liked to express their affection physically and that sex was fun I was initially revolted. The diagrams in my school biology book confirmed my repulsion. Far from encouraging me to go on out there and do it, her well-meaning efforts put me off (for a couple of years). Probably the effect she was after. Another girlfriend of mine was on the verge of losing her virginity at fifteen until her mother showed her an illustrated book on sexually transmitted diseases. As a direct result she became a fellatio expert but refused to have full sex until she was approaching twenty. Her theory being that at least with oral sex you got to scrutinise the article first. She also credits it as being the reason all her exes are still in love with her. So, well done her mum on both counts.

I'm all for delaying the moment that young people embark on sexual relationships for as long as possible. With so much angst and pain and confusion to deal with in your teens the intensity of premature sex only adds to the clutter. Nevertheless I'm a realist and the fact is that most kids these days have had sex by the time they're fifteen, let alone nineteen. There's a moral minority that still believes that this is the result of sex education in schools. No teenager I've ever met, boy or girl, has intimated their desire for children except in the far future; yet we live in a country with more teenage pregnancies than anywhere else in Europe. You don't have to be a detective to establish that there's a lot of ignorance out there. These fruitcakes would have us believe that showing children approaching their teens computer-generated diagrams on how male/female sexual organs work together in one of the only moments of symmetry between the sexes is enough to have them flying out of the door and into the arms of the nearest pimply stranger.

Perhaps I lack imagination? How do these diagrams of little tadpole sperms swimming along a (generally flesh-pink) channel until finally the lucky winner arrives at Mummy's egg work like pornography for the under-sixteen's? Without instruction teenagers are still well aware of sex. How could they not be? Sex is all around these days, from *Big Brother* to *Buffy the Vampire Slayer*, *Heat* magazine to the *Sun*. And seldom in any way connected to love. I don't want to come across as an old fogey hippy, but isn't that the most important lesson to learn about the sexual act? And who better to learn it from than your parents?

There's a huge difference between sexual awareness and sexual understanding. What you should be telling your daughter is that she's sharing something very precious with her boyfriend, that it would be lovely if they stayed together but they probably won't (she'll scream in protestation at the latter) and that she should always remember sex is not something she ever needs to feel pressured into doing. One of the worst aspects of teenage sexual awakening as a girl is that boys make you feel that you owe them sex for getting them all hot and bothered in the first place. What nobody explains is that teenage boys are at such a hormonal pitch that a Polaroid of Margaret Thatcher's knickers would probably push them over the edge. A state that some Tory MPs don't mature out of, I've heard.

I suggest you tell your daughter it's a deal . . . with a few provisos. First that you and she go out for a long walk together. Then you work up the courage to have a frank exchange with her on the subject of love and sex. You also tell her that she can sleep with her boyfriend provided she observes the etiquette that you and her father have throughout her short life. It's a private activity between two people, and you don't want to hear her wails of pleasure, have the two of them making tongue sandwiches in the kitchen or occupying each other and the sofa in an arrogant teenage sprawl. Explain that it's hard as a parent, seeing the little creature you gave birth to and have had sole access to on the kissing and cuddling front suddenly only wanting to be loved by some spotty stranger. Let her know that she is your cherished little girl. If you can talk to her about what's important now you'll open a communication channel that will stand you in good stead all your lives.

I'm Dreading the Parting

My boyfriend, who I've been dating for a year, is going to live in Australia in a couple of months. He's just thirty and I knew when we first met he was going to leave, but as it looms ever closer I feel increasingly scared. Meanwhile I've also had a bit of a fling with an ex who lives with his new girlfriend. All I want is a steady relationship. I'm nearly forty. So should I finish it now with my man to minimise future heartache or is that being selfish?

There he is trying to deal with the emotional wrench of saying goodbye to his current life and all you're worried about is yourself. Of course it's going to hurt like hell when he goes, but is splitting up with him now going to hurt any less? You're an adult woman and you made a choice to embark on a relationship in full knowledge of his imminent departure. I think you ought to develop a bit of personal responsibility. Or at least display the courage of your convictions. You were happy to date him despite the fact that he was leaving (we'll get on to that in a moment), by the sound of things he hasn't stopped treating you well, the relationship is not suffering anything other than collateral damage, so for heaven's sake give him the send-off he deserves. It's not his fault that you're so petrified of commitment that you do everything in your power to avoid a real relationship.

I suspect you don't need to me to illuminate you on the subtext of your actions, just to confirm what you've already realised. Each new decade brings its problems but if you anticipate them and start preparing then you can at least minimise their impact. Forty is a great age to start making radical changes. I'm sure you're telling me your age, completely irrelevant in the situation you're describing, because you want to address the bigger picture but are afraid to put it into words. What is a woman approaching her forties doing dating a man ten years younger who's leaving the country? Ten years younger and lives next door on the other hand is an excellent idea. Age does matter: at yours you should be preparing for a future, not stuck in a *Groundhog Day*-style present where every relationship results in the same empty void.

You say you were seeing an ex who has a girlfriend – have you no sense as well as no pride? It reminds me of a well-to-do friend of mine who refuses to go to the sales. Her reasoning being that she has no intention of rushing around buying up the things nobody else wanted! Weren't you doing the same thing in reverse, conducting a relationship with someone who had made his choice and it wasn't you? That's going to do a lot for a girl's ego and self-confidence now, isn't it? He didn't even have short-term security to offer.

You're at an age where you can choose to use your life experience positively, or behave like the proverbial ostrich, head buried deep in the sand, feigning surprise when you reach fifty that your life hasn't changed. Do you really want to spend what many women describe as their favourite decade stuck in an easily escapable rut while all around you people are learning from their mistakes and moving on? You need to develop a whole new attitude to dating. If he's otherwise involved, lives abroad, is still a bachelor at eighty, thinks he might be gay, or is about to embark on a new life elsewhere, he's not for you. That sort of thing is fine in your twenties and early thirties but you don't have time to sit around and wait for someone to leave their partner or realise they can't survive the outback without you.

Not that I'm suggesting you turn into one of those thirty-somethings one of my siblings described with horror the other day. Women so eager to find a long-term partner that they virtually conduct a job interview on the first date. Putting attitudes to children, career potential, past relationships and future prospects under Mossad-style scrutiny before you've even ordered the hors d'oeuvres. It's enough to destroy any appetite, sexual or culinary, in one fell swoop. No relationship arrives gift-wrapped, pristine and blemish-free, particularly post your teens. It's unlikely you'll meet a partner with everything you desire ready to be ticked off as perfect in every category.

However, there is a happy medium, and you, my friend, are not making life easy for yourself. See off your current beau with dignity and strength; show him how marvellous the older woman is! Then take a sabbatical for a couple of months to lick your wounds, after which you should set out, brimful of resolve not to settle for anything less than your heart's desire. A committed relationship that you can grow old and mellow with. You've already hinted that you can see your pattern, so throw that design out the window and create a whole new one. Your future is in your hands: stop taking time out in futile attempts to hide from it.

I'm Tempted to Stray

I am in my late forties and I have to admit, until recently, I'd let myself go to seed a bit. My wife's nagging finally got me to my local tennis club – tennis being a sport I used to enjoy immensely – and now I'm there two evenings a week and feel fitter and stronger as a result. The problem is I have developed a friendship with a member of my tennis group, a woman, and although it is still at a platonic level I'm worried that it might go further. I don't know if I can trust my feelings for this woman. She is younger than my wife, a divorcee and very attractive.

You haven't been keeping your eye on the ball now, have you? But first let me congratulate you. So many men just settle in and welcome the rot, gazing affectionately at their beer bellies, and in confusion at the puny matchsticks that once carried them down a football field and now barely get them up the stairs at night. You've actually gone out there and done something about it. So many of us faced with the indisputable evidence of our bodies' slow decline sit back and treat it like a peep show. It's a pleasure akin to 'rubbernecking' at traffic accidents. Instead of stopping to help, or continuing straight ahead, we succumb to the tantalising lure of glimpsing something gruesome, repelled and fascinated in equal measure. It's the same with our bodies: instead of taking action, or ignoring them completely, we tend to look on helplessly as we fall apart. I always remember a photograph of Fergie, Duchess of York that endeared me to her no end. She lay on a sun-lounger, gazing with morbid fascination at the fistful of cellulite she'd managed to grab on her thigh. It was a deliciously human moment.

It's a dangerous thing to let middle age wash over you in a tidal wave of indolence. For so long our bodies just play along while we take them for granted. We stock them up with alcohol and coffee and cigarettes, crunching them up with bad posture, and then one day when the back gives in, the knees start to crumble, or the flab wraps itself like a duvet around your once skeletal frame, you know it's too late. Such lethargy is not to be encouraged. We should be pulling out our swords and doing battle with nature and her cruel plans, pushing her ever backwards, not inviting her around for a cup of tea and then asking her to move in. It's no coincidence that our reluctance to 'rage, rage against the dying of the light' and the dying of the light itself tend to collide.

Unrestrained, our bodies will hurtle recklessly towards disintegration, both mentally and physically. We need to take out a restraining order against decline. Refuse to let it into our immediate vicinity and ignore its presence if it manages to creep up behind us. Those still energetic in their latter years are frequently the people whose natural inclination has been to devour life in great gobfuls; when they see life about to get its own back they take it on, chin up, chest out. As Shakespeare pointed out, it may be inevitable that 'Golden lads and girls all must, as chimney-sweepers come to dust' but there's no need to give in without a fight.

As we were told about the Iraq War, it's a battle that must begin before the enemy has made his first move. Otherwise it's not just your body, but also your soul that sinks into decline. If you start to feel physically defeated you will be less energetic at work and positively lethargic at home. Which brings me back to you. I've got a feeling you are confusing endorphins with the first stirring of love.

It's an easy mistake to make. The fresh blood coursing through your veins is bound to make you feel vital and even sexy.

So you're right to question your feelings for this woman. I'm sure she is very attractive, and thanks to your newfound zest you have managed to register that. She has everything to gain and nothing to lose. You on the other hand would be losing a valuable relationship in which I imagine you have much invested. Here you are being given an added extension to your life and what are you about to do? Throw away the old one even though there was nothing wrong with it. It's hardly fair for this stranger to reap the benefits of your renewed 'lust for life' when it was your wife who recognised the symptoms of decay and helped you reverse them in the first place.

We're all so obsessed with the new that we forget that, with minimal effort, we can have a brand-new experience with the same person, in the same place, at the same time. Moving on isn't necessarily moving up. Use all that fresh new blood pumping through your veins to invigorate your marriage, not destroy it. If the temptation to stray proves too much at your local tennis club I suggest you take up a same-sex sport. You certainly won't be confusing those endorphins with true love on a rugby pitch.

Is It Selfish Not to Want Children?

Is it OK not to want children? Society suggests otherwise.
My husband and his family keep making pointed remarks
about the pattering of tiny feet. Just the other day my
mother-in-law insinuated that I shouldn't have got married
if I wasn't prepared to procreate. I can't quite face telling
them the truth – that I value my lifestyle and my freedom
and don't want to give them up. Am I just being selfish?

The in-laws are always right! Seriously. To baby or not to
baby? – It's a difficult question. Choice is a wonderful
thing; or at least knowing you've got one is. In my experience actually making a choice has far less to recommend
it. It's hard enough to try and decide whether to go for
chicken or meat on an aeroplane, nigh impossible to deter-
mine with any confidence when or if to bring another life
into the world. First and foremost I suggest you relax.
Society and your in-laws can think what they like. Frankly
it's none of anyone else's business. Apart from your
husband, that is. Your mother-in-law has a point to her
advantage on that score. I'm curious as to why you didn't
have this conversation before you married. He of all people
surely had the right to know you didn't care to bear children? Which is why I'm wondering if you are as adamant
about it as you are trying to sound.

I've yet to meet a woman so overcome with broodiness
that she was swaying to the beat of her internal tick-tock.
If anything, desperation to have a child is reserved for those
poor couples struggling to achieve conception for medical
reasons and neurotic singletons who want to add an extra

worry to their list. It's like glancing at a Kit-Kat when you're on a diet. Suddenly it goes from being a fairly average chocolate bar to the most delectable delicacy on earth. The same goes for having babies. If you can have them you're not sure you want them; if you can't, having them becomes an obsession.

It's instilled in girls from an early age that one day they're going to wake up and feel such excruciating pangs to procreate that nothing short of a cement chastity belt will keep them from pregnancy. Maybe that was true fifty years ago when anything looked more appealing that dusting the house for the seventh time that week. Nowadays few women experience that Damascene moment, so you are not alone.

There is certainly a clock ticking, and being pragmatists most women are perfectly well aware of it. The question is what to do about it. The number of mothers in their forties has doubled in the last decade. There's no mystery as to why. They work hard, achieve what they can and suddenly time's running out so they give conception their best shot. In many cases it's not a considered choice but one forced on women afraid of losing their right to choose. One moment you're nervously preparing for your first job interview, the next you're in your late thirties listening to a gynaecologist tell you that your chances of conceiving are a mere 5 per cent.

I suspect you're not yet approaching forty. If you are then I accept you really don't want children. If you're not I advise you to keep an open mind. Independence and pleasing yourself can seem a lot less appealing when fifty is closer than twenty. Just now you're kept awake by nightmares about being pregnant. Just wait until they metamorphose into the hot flush of menopause that signals the end of that choice. Not that I'm trying to employ the sort of scare tactics your mother-in-law might try. I'm just saying that fabulous, flighty, independent lifestyles can lose their sparkle when the body indulging in them is no longer in its youthful prime.

I don't think it's a question of how much you love your husband. Could it however be a form of punishment for the sacrifice in lifestyle you feel you made by marrying him? Having a baby will of course have a dramatic impact on your life. A friend who had been eager to have a child told me the other day that she is still, six years later, reeling from the shock of motherhood. According to her it was friends who imagined the worst who found the experience less dramatic. At least you would fall into that bracket!

Are you just digging in your heels because you feel bullied? If you really love your partner and it's that important to him you'll have to consider it or consider passing him on to someone else. Surely first there's a discussion to be had about how it would be approached, who'd do the majority of the child-minding, and so on.

Finally, if you really don't want to have a baby it is your choice; one you should maybe have informed your husband of before you married him, but your choice nonetheless. Don't abuse it. Use it wisely. It's one of the great gifts of being a woman and not one to be turned down lightly.

I'm Useless with Girls

I'm twenty years old and recently stumbled on your column in my dad's newspaper. My problem is girls. I get on great with all the women at my office but in a social situation I am useless. I recently broke up with someone I work with and it's not been easy seeing her every day. I don't want to end up in the same situation again. Can you help? By the way, judging by your picture you're not bad-looking yourself. Don't worry – that's not a come-on!

Phew, for a minute I was really scared! I'm delighted that you stumbled across me in your *father's* paper – you really know how to make a woman feel middle-aged. My first suggestion is that for our sake you don't start dating older women. We're after confidence-building, not decimation. You don't say why you split with your last girlfriend but could it be because she discovered that you didn't have anything in common apart from work? You say that it's there that you're most confident. This suggests that you haven't developed interests and opinions of your own. It's a mistake we make very easily these days and it's not confined to the young. Within seconds of an introduction it's considered fair game to question a person on their occupation. Depending on the answer we imagine that somehow we've taken a short cut to their soul. Or at least can now place them in a convenient category. Accountant – boring, lawyer – boring and unscrupulous, politician – boring, vain and sleazy, journalist – boring, vain, sleazy and unscrupulous, celebrity – absolutely fabulous and fascinating, and so it continues.

In some countries, arguably on this point more cultured

than our own, it's considered the height of bad manners to question a person on their occupation until you know them better. My best friend lives in Italy and as a result of my regular visits to see her I've been introduced to a whole group of people I only see briefly twice or three times a year. Most of them I've now known casually for years and yet it's only recently that I've become aware of their occupations. Latin countries, more famous for their quality of life than their GDP, consider the hours outside work to be of paramount importance. I'd certainly exchange Top Dog Nation status and its by-products (traffic, road rage and stress) for a little less in the Bank of England Reserve and a little more quality of life.

In the UK we're getting closer to America every day, not just in Tony's toadying to Bush on Iraq but also in terms of how we judge people. Success attracts success and failure is as repulsive as leprosy (and treated as equally contagious). Perhaps it's time we studied the way we qualify those two categories? If I clamber to the pinnacle of fame and fortune and in the process leave all that I love behind, have I succeeded or failed? If I'm flat broke and out of work but surrounded by goodness and love, am I not the better off?

Philosophy, the discipline that asks these big questions, is enjoying a rebirth at present. We may not yet be breeding new Socrates and Kierkegaards, but academics like A.C. Grayling and Alain de Botton have both written best-selling and easily digestible guides to a richer inner life. No wonder we're starting to look within for answers. We're like the spoilt offspring of wealthy parents. So used to having everything we thought we needed that we've no idea how to enjoy it.

So frenetic has the pace of modern life become that more and more people are opting for something simpler, even if

63

being poorer (financially) is part of the compromise. What purpose is there to spending forty years working flat out, destroying relationships and childhoods in the process, just to be able to play out the final twenty on a Costa del Sol golf course. It's not hobbies that we need but a decent reason for continuing as a species. Fished out, farmed out, cynical, lethargic about the legacy we're bequeathing, we're a pretty dismal bunch. And still we race on, trying to keep our eyes focused straight ahead and our confidence topped up. What harm if we paused one day and took a little look around? The answers we're looking for aren't to be found in magazines, self-help books or as a result of a pay rise. Our knee-jerk response to the perceived pressure of modern life is an ill-considered sprint towards a future day where we'll have everything we thought we ever wanted . . . and nothing we needed at all.

You may think I've gone off at the deep end. After all, you're only twenty years old. You're not supposed to be looking at the big picture, unless it's at your local multiplex, but it's never too early to embrace what's important in life. It seems that you're not a regular reader of your father's paper. I suspect you're not a regular reader at all. Perhaps you ought to give it a shot. I know rebellion is all about doing the opposite of your parents, so buy the *Telegraph* and really piss him off. You need to find a world outside your office where you can be in control of your own destiny and confident of your thoughts. It's there you'll find both the reason for your lack of confidence and the cure.

I suspect for you the road to happiness lies in moulding yourself into a person you find interesting. Try books, films, woodwork, sky-diving. Kick-start the journey to becoming a fully rounded human being who doesn't rely on life's accessories to define him. I'm glad you are already questioning yourself. It shows that you have much to offer the world, but first you have to find your place in it. After that talking to girls will be a breeze. If you blossom into a man who understands himself, has considered opinions and is still eager to learn, you'll not just be talking to girls, you'll be swatting them off.

I'm Dreading His Stag Weekend

My boyfriend and I recently decided to get married. We've been living together for the last ten years and have two young children. We made the decision to tie the knot on a rare weekend away from the kids! Before it had never seemed a priority and also he's been married once before. The problem is, money is a bit tight and he's insisting on a stag weekend in Amsterdam with a bunch of his mates. Am I being a spoilsport for not wanting him to go?

If you're a spoilsport, so am I. Hasn't he heard that the Dutch police are cracking down on the scores of idiots roaming their city, moaning about the impending crisis of marriage and behaving like they've just escaped from a dark cave? I'm constantly amazed at the long leash men expect as some kind of compensation for giving up their 'freedom'. The general consensus seems to be, 'All right, love, I'm prepared to turn my back on the fantastic, commitment-free, babe-filled life I could be leading in order to make you happy. But before I do that I need to bugger off and sleep with a couple of hookers after spending a month's wages on getting wasted with my mates.' Reasonable, or what?

This whole stag-night culture needs re-examining. In these supposedly more enlightened days, do we really still accept that prior to 'settling down' with the one they love every man needs a night or two of behaving like a regressed Neanderthal? Having sown all his 'wild oats' in one night he'll find his future crop will be of the domestic porridge oats variety. It really beggars belief that modern women are still buying into this line in a completely misguided act of gratitude for getting their boyfriends to commit.

I'm not gearing up to some feminist rant when I say that the person making the major sacrifice in a marriage is generally speaking the woman; just repeating the facts. Statistics show 90 per cent of men are happiest when married, while with women the opposite is true. If anyone needs to disappear for twenty-four hours and have the kind of hedonistic sex that only money can buy it's the wife in waiting. The trouble is that if they do they end up looking as smutty and redundant as their blokes. There's only one thing worse than a bawdy stag night and that's a hen night trying to be a bawdy stag night. Don't get me wrong – I'm all for single-sex gatherings. I just don't see why they can't be a regular occurrence rather than a last desperate punt at singledom before we get hitched.

The irony is that it's not just the bride to be that dreads such gatherings. Most intelligent men groan in trepidation at the horrors they're going to face in giving their mate the expected send-off. I recall recently a male friend whose planned stag night sounded like an extremely civilised affair. Ten of his best friends in a rented country mansion for a weekend of clay shooting, dirt-bike riding and other manly pursuits. The Friday night was a great success, tales of great embarrassment to the groom were related, much whisky was drunk and they all stumbled to bed in the wee hours. The next night two of the ten, army officers I'm afraid to say, became obsessed with the idea that no stag weekend would be complete without the obligatory stripper. They spent the early evening browsing the local Yellow Pages until they finally struck gold with an escort agency. A small miracle in this rural area.

The rest of the guys experienced feelings ranging from slight trepidation to outright discomfort at the idea. Their fears turned to terror when the lady in question arrived looking more like Camilla Parker-Bowles than Jordan. It was Gloucestershire after all. As she writhed on the ancient oak dining table in her red nylon stockings and suspenders to the tune of 'Ooh Micky, ah Micky' the majority of guests were as embarrassed as if it had been their own mother. Meanwhile the two officers were bellowing to the groom to get involved. He ended up knocking one of them out as he battled to escape.

Then again I heard a story about a father of two, who decided after three years of marriage and seven years together to reward himself with a wild weekend in Ayiah Napa. Instead of just telling his wife he wanted a weekend away he employed emotional blackmail by insisting it was the stag night he'd never had. They'd married on the spur of the moment while on holiday. Off he set for two days with the friends who agreed to accompany him. A couple of them thought the whole thing too ridiculous to indulge. On his return he discovered that his wife and kids were spending the weekend at her sister's in the country. Furious that she wasn't there to greet him, he telephoned and demanded she come home. I wish I could tell you that she told him where to get off.

Twenty-first-century stag nights are a travesty that fails to live up to any scrutiny. They hail back to an era when marriage meant the first time you had sex with your bride, the last time you had sex with anyone else and the embarkation point for an entirely different way of living. This is no longer true. Most couples enjoy a healthy mix of independence and codependence so they're really not waving goodbye to very much.

Then there's the fact that (as your partner knows full well) marriage often doesn't last for ever. When planning a second and third trip to the registry office you can't seriously keep a straight face when insisting on your divine right to kiss goodbye to singledom; again. If marriage sometimes looks like an outdated institution then the traditional stag night is positively prehistoric. I suggest you tell him he can go on a weekend away with his mates any time he likes. Just so long as he doesn't mention the word stag night.

My Girlfriend's Too Fat

My problem is an ancient one. My girlfriend has put on weight and although she's always been a bit above average I'm now starting to find her less attractive. I recently ran the marathon and lost a lot of weight during my training programme. I don't understand why she can't get up off her bum and go to the gym. I feel really good now that I'm fit and toned. Perhaps I should split up with her and give her the incentive to go on a diet?

An age-old situation? I'm not so sure. It's only in the last century that looking like a half-starved anorexic has become something to boast about. You say your girlfriend has an 'above-average' figure. What, might I ask, is average? In this country alone 63 per cent of the population is overweight; in America the figure is much higher. So your girlfriend's weight is above average for where

exactly? Sloane Street? Notting Hill? Glasgow Central? I suspect that in some areas of the country (and city), where chip shops and kebab outlets replace salad bars, designer coffee bars and organic superstores, your girlfriend would probably be regarded as the local Jodie Kidd. On the island of Tonga in the South Seas, where weight is positively celebrated, they'd probably force-feed her. Nevertheless I agree you do have a problem. I'm just not sure that it's your girlfriend's weight.

Are you sure your girlfriend hasn't become a mirror? You're not seeing *her*, rather your scary old fat self reflected back at you in your girlfriend's 'above-average' frame. Often the thing we nag our partners about most, whether it's drinking, flirting, over-eating or potential adultery, is often the very thing we're most prone to ourselves. I can't help feeling that this is personal. It sounds to me that whenever you look at her you feel the anger, frustration and loathing that you feel for yourself. I don't want to get all Freudian about it, but how was your childhood? Your anger about her not making the effort is palpable.

Her weight doesn't seem to have been a problem before. She must be so grateful that she was given dispensation to be a porker until you decided to reinvent yourself as Brad Pitt. I'm impressed that you've taken the plunge and decided to do something proactive about your own hang-up. But frankly, don't expect the rest of the world to start tapping their toes to your tune. Maybe you are trying to find an excuse to get out of the relationship. Have you lost interest in your girlfriend? These days you probably like to spend evenings hanging out with your new gym buddies comparing pecs and drinking Red Bulls. Meanwhile she's at home munching through a box of Celebrations and wishing she had a boyfriend who made her feel sexy.

The thing about weight is that it never is about weight. We all eat our way up and down the scales depending on our hormones, our happiness, our access to healthy food, our mental state, and our romantic status. Your girlfriend might well lose weight if you dumped her. But it's a risky route to take. You wouldn't necessarily be welcomed back into her now *ET*-like arms when the pounds dropped off. Most likely you'd discover some new bloke balanced precariously on her newly razor-sharp hip bones. Or indeed the converse might occur. Losing a 'well-toned' guy like you might drive her to an orgy of gluttony. Next thing you knew she'd be a pin-up on the cover of the *Sunday Sport* or 'Fat Birds' monthly.

You perhaps naively believe that there is some sort of body-weight norm that exists. I can assure you that this is not the case. Some men really don't want a hard-bodied trampoline in their bed. If you don't like the person you're with, stop judging her so harshly and making her feel insecure. Just move on.

Then again you might love her to pieces and just wish she was a little skinnier. In which case the first thing you need to do is make her feel sexy and gorgeous. Confidence makes people blossom. You can help to restore or destroy hers. If she feels well loved she won't be reaching for the snack tray. Try positive action. You need to inspire your girlfriend into getting fit, not goad her to despair (via the fridge). Going to the gym isn't the only way to lose weight. Try and think of something she might actually enjoy. Go for a weekend walking in some remote beauty spot; make it challenging and romantic. Or take up some kind of physical exercise as a hobby and entice her along. Cycling, or tennis, or jogging, or yoga, or swimming. Slimming isn't about the burn: it's about the brain. Use yours and I bet you'll defeat her lethargy.

I'm Losing My Best Friend

R. and I have been friends for twenty years, sometimes close, sometimes more distant, but always like a rock for each other. We are both forty and bisexual. Last January, her partner died suddenly, after nine years together – a loss intensified as she had also lost her father the year before. She is now without family, save for a sister she does not see eye to eye with.

Basically my problem is that this death has created a gulf between us, because, despite knowing pain, suffering and loneliness (i.e., being human), I have never known the territory she now inhabits. Although I try to reach her it feels like waving at someone on the moon. This feels scary, I feel I need her beside me, to keep her safe. Odd thing to say, but I just need to know she's OK, and not sinking.

The problem is, like any person in grief, she is monumentally selfish. I have filed a countless number of rebuffs and hurts under 'making allowances'. But how do you know when to stop making allowances? I am always asking her does she want me to do x, y or z for her, but more often than not the answer is an abrupt no. The most recent (and hurtful): I asked her if she wanted to spend part of Christmas day with me – I'm married with two young kids.

This is a toughie. Although you think you have your friend's best interests at heart it's worth examining your own motives. You say you need to keep her close in order to know she's safe; how do you propose to do that? After all, even if she'd been umbilically attached to you it wouldn't have prevented her losing the two people closest to her.

You probably think I'm being pedantic by picking on such details but they are all I have with which to create a relief map of your emotional terrain. Perhaps this current impasse is more about you than you think?

Friendship is such a complex emotional relationship. I think sometimes we forget just what a minefield it can be. The common view is that friendship is based on simple criteria: shared interests, similar backgrounds, geographical proximity and compatible lifestyles. Of course all these are contributing factors but ultimately, selfish beings that we are, the friendships we make tend to reflect our various stages of development. This is fine if you're talking about the 'new best friend' syndrome to which even the worthiest among us is susceptible, but hard if you've known each other half your lives. The NBF is generally a socially driven union, which is as seductive and compelling as it is transient. Not that there is anything wrong with that sort of bonding; it's great fun and it's part of our development. The problem is that often the strength of friendship is defined, particularly by women, by its intensity. So any relationship not living up to that frenetic level of interchange is judged to be somehow lacking. I'm not so sure that we use the correct barometer.

Daily communication can actually be the enemy of real conversation, as anyone in a long-term relationship will no doubt concur. Trivia helps the words flow but gets in the way of saying anything that matters. The much more natural condition for friendship in a world that is never static is one of ebb and flow. Our lives are punctuated by the arrival, departure and return of true friends who never desert us – they just take occasional mini-breaks. Some consider this unacceptable behaviour; others see such tolerance as the true definition of friendship. I'm in the latter camp. In fact I'm suspicious of people who measure the depth of their connection by the frequency of the communication. Good friends don't scream if you don't call back; confident of their place in your affections they're happy to give you space. Sometimes the people closest to you are those you only turn to in crisis, which by its very nature doesn't happen that often.

So I suggest you should relax about R. It's possible that your well-meaning offers to do 'x, y or z' for her (instead of 'with her') only unbalance the relationship and make her feel worse. You are her friend, not a nursemaid. Neither does she want you struggling to reach her depths of despair. Instead your position should be at the water's edge, carrying a rubber ring in the event of an emergency. If she turns down your invitations it's not personal unless you make it so. My guess is that she's not up to your level of engagement; not ready to take up your invitations and suggestions. It doesn't mean she's not your friend, she's just coping the best way she can.

You're the one with a problem. You need to know that she needs you. Maybe she doesn't; maybe she just likes you? Can you cope with that new role? My guess is you should give her space. Let her know you care, tell her you'll be there when she's ready but you are going to stop trying to save her. Everyone has a different way of coping and she's trying to get on with hers.

As for Christmas, I wouldn't be too hurt. Being bystander to your domestic bliss is probably a little too much at present for your mate in mourning. Let her go, and then you'll get to watch her bounce back.

What's Wrong with Gay Marriage?

My partner and I want to get married. After sixteen years, we are still very much in love and want to make that commitment to each other – but we are gay. Why is it illegal for us to marry? People quote the Bible but in the Bible it's also forbidden to eat prawns and no one gets arrested for that. It seems unfair that our relationship is considered less stable than that of two teenagers who've been together a few weeks.

You have a point and I think you know it. Marriage is in such trouble these days that the government should be doing everything in their power to revive the institution. I'd suggest subsidies and incentives but they don't seem to have done much for the film industry. Perhaps the answer

is to throw the doors wide open and let every Tom, Dick and Harry enjoy a stroll up the aisle or into the registry office like the rest of us. And let's not forget that there'd be Kate and Sadie and Saffron and all our sapphic friends queuing up as well. Encouraging those previously left on the fringes of society, whose sexual leanings leave them in a catch-22 situation where they are tolerated but deemed unworthy of society's blessing, would provide a much needed injection of life into a tradition which is quite frankly struggling to survive. Not only would lovely stable relationships like yours provide valuable role models, they would also potentially quadruple the number of marriages taking place. I'm all for it and if they held a referendum tomorrow I'd be more than happy to place my cross in the relevant box.

Before you go popping off to Holland or Denmark to tie the knot give the matter some careful consideration. Don't you find it a little curious that so many gay relationships enjoy a longevity and stability envied by many less fortunate heterosexuals? Maybe your relationship is successful precisely because of everyone else's low expectations of it. I'm not saying that it isn't a lovely thing to pledge your love for each other in front of the people who matter in your lives. I'm presuming *Hello!* and *OK* wouldn't be present? But you have followed your heart and your sexuality into pastures less trammelled. Look around and you'll see plenty of couples less fortunate.

I've always thought that a bit of Dunkirk spirit does wonders for a relationship. Whether it's parental disapproval, inter-racial condemnation, friends who're convinced you're ill-matched, obnoxious exes forever butting in, or the disapproval of middle England as a whole, couples seem to consolidate in the face of adversity.

Often in these dysfunctional days families are made up of people we try to avoid, neighbours are nameless spectres who leave their TV turned up too loud, and work colleagues are hard to miss, thanks to the large knife they're waving in the vicinity of our backs. Who wants them dolled up and enjoying free drinks at your expense when you could be cuddled up at home enjoying *Maurice* on video?

Whether you're for or against marriage as an institution there's no denying that it's hardly a recipe for success in a relationship these days. The statistics make dismal reading. It seems that the moment we get society to sit up and take notice of our blooming love affair, or at least accept its validity in the eyes of the law, the petals start falling off. I heard about a dinner party the other day that resulted in not one but four divorces. The first couple disintegrated at the discovery (mid-dinner) of one partner's infidelity. The rest collapsed like skittles during the following weeks. Their relationships had become so reliant on the social framework of acceptable coupledom that the minute a piece was removed the whole lot tumbled. It was as if they'd been playing relationship Jenga. This is the volatile territory into which you aspire to thrust your happy, stable and apparently idyllic partnership. I admit there are long-term financial securities afforded by pairing up in the eyes of the law. They can also be arranged with the services of a good lawyer.

The trouble with modern marriage is that it's built with balsa wood. An unexpected breeze and the whole thing collapses. You and your lover have proved that your relationship is built of much stronger stuff. You don't need a rubber stamp of approval from anyone, least of all bureaucratic strangers, in order to maintain an adult, loving, well-functioning union of two like-minded souls. I'm curious as to why you're looking to the ailing institution of marriage to support a relationship that doesn't seem to need any scaffolding.

My Ex-husband Should Buy Me a Flat

I've recently split up with my husband of four years. He and I just don't get on and I want my freedom back. When we married I sold my small flat and moved in with him. I've spent most of the money I made on my property on clothes and little extras for myself. Since I need somewhere to live and he earns double my salary surely he should buy me a flat?

Surely not! Obviously it's hard to judge your input into the relationship from those brief lines but it sounds to me like you've wasted away your own cash and now you expect him to pay. I read in a newspaper the other day about a new group of females called Sarahs. Single and rich and happy. Perhaps you're planning to join them? Their happiness is explained by the presence of £25,000 plus in their bank accounts gleaned not from hard labour but unsuccessful journeys down the aisle. Women are often accused of having it all. An absolute nonsense, as any working mother, harassed housewife or lonely singleton will tell you. Nevertheless when it comes to marriage we can certainly be accused of *wanting* it all. Independence, equality, our own income, and then when we lose interest in our partner half of what he's got too. It's a horrible trend, and like chewing gum, fast food and nylon sportswear, has sneaked its way across the Atlantic courtesy of our American cousins. In their litigious world everything has a price and love is increasingly subject to rampant inflation. These Sarahs give the ordinary divorcee seeking only what is rightfully his or hers a bad name. They seem to have confused marriage with the more accepted way of earning money for sex: namely, prostitution.

I had a heated argument with one of my best friends about this subject just the other day. We were driving home from the country and passing the time we got on to the trials and tribulations of mutual friends who are divorcing. He's better aquainted with the husband, I with the bride. But I think our points of view were informed more by the male/female divide than by our relationships with those concerned.

The way I see it, my girlfriend put up with years of abject hell. She was a legal-aid lawyer who loved her job, but she wasn't getting any younger. She and her husband really wanted kids and he was one of the few lucky Internet entrepreneurs. In other words he was rich. He longed for a semi-rural life, so she decided to give up work and attempt to make his dreams come true. They set themselves up in the country and he commuted to London three days a week. By all accounts marriage didn't interfere with his fun while he was in the metropolis. I was often told salacious stories about his ribald nights out with the boys, and although I have no definite proof there is plenty of evidence to suggest he wasn't faithful. Not that I'm taking any high moral ground. These are faithless days and we're all open to a bit of temptation. In fact I even partly blame my friend, his wife, who took her country retirement very seriously and refused to accompany him to town for all but the most unavoidable of situations.

Her husband was delighted to have a 'real' home to recharge his batteries in and kept lecturing her single girl-friends (me included) on how our selfish ways were the cause of society's rot. To cut a long story short, after six years in the sticks, with his trips to town becoming more frequent rather than less, the marriage fell apart. Instead of bringing them together their attempt at 'the good life' had left them leading completely different lives. Perhaps if they'd had children things would have been different but they'd been unlucky on the conception front and she wanted back into the working world.

He was devastated. Painting London red started to feel like the empty experience he'd deep down suspected it was, and back in the country he found himself wandering listlessly from room to room with no one but their cats for company. Meanwhile she'd taken a tiny flat in London and had managed to get a part-time job in a local legal practice. She was broke but said she felt like herself again for the first time in years. So began the divorce proceedings.

Which brings me back to you. My girlfriend sued him for a quarter of his fortune. My driving companion felt this was outrageous. It was typical of the modern woman to expect recompense for her decision to quit work and take care of her husband. His responsibility to her ended the minute she walked out the door. She made the decision to give up work and neither that, nor the fact that she'd failed to conceive (his words) were her husband's responsibility. I was shocked by his attitude but not surprised. Acres of column inches are devoted annually to the exploits of female gold-diggers. He was just tarring my friend with the same brush. Yet here was a woman who'd happily looked after herself financially for years, had given up her independence in order to advance her husband's career and was now at forty-plus having to start again from scratch. She hadn't run off with anybody else, had played second fiddle to her hubby for six years, and now just wanted a fair share of what I think should be regarded as mutual earnings.

My friend said I was just being a rabid feminist manhater who felt all men should pay. That's just not true.

Each case has to be judged on its individual merits. For example, I think you've got a bit of a cheek. If we're equal at work and equal at play then when relationships go wrong we can't expect to revert to being helpless little women. I'm hoping this story will put your own relationship in perspective. The situation you find yourself in is not the same. The problem for my soon-to-be-divorced girlfriend is that her perfectly legitimate pursuit of what is rightfully hers has been demeaned by women like you. You seem to believe that what's yours is yours and what's his is yours.

In the old days women buttoned their lips and stayed the course because the alternative was non-existent. Nowadays you can walk out the door, get in your car, book a singles holiday and then get back to the dating game. Instead of expecting your ex to subsidise your newly single life, dust off the purchases you frittered your savings on and use them to lure a new boyfriend. And next time around rent out your flat!

What's the Point of Working?

I am a twenty-six-year-old marine engineer. I live with my girlfriend in a one-bedroom flat, which we bought just before property prices took off. I am in a bit of a mess, though. I hate my job/career and cannot see a way out.

I have never had job satisfaction. In fact I can't remember the last time I was satisfied with anything I have done. Achieving my degree gave me mild satisfaction but more a sense of relief in that I had finished it. I don't really want to work – it's not just that I'm lazy, it's that work seems so pointless: get out of bed every day at the same time, go and sit behind the same desk until the end of the day, go home, eat, sleep, and get up and do it all again . . . for forty years.

I am looking for a quick fix. I don't want to be a millionaire – I just don't want to go to work. I'd be really happy to be a beach bum again like I was in my year out. I worked as a windsurfing instructor, teaching during the day, windsurfing in my spare time and getting rat-arsed in the

evening. What's the point of going to work to pay the mortgage when I know there are all those fantastic beaches out
there with warm blue seas and plenty of windsurfing to do?
So, as you can see, I am pretty confused . . .

My, that's a strong gust of existential angst blowing in from
the West Country. Who am I? Why am I here? What's the
point? Poor you, faced with forty years of desk-bound
drudgery. But haven't you stepped right over the middle
ground? You are young, healthy and solvent. If you want
to pack up and work on cirrhosis of the liver instead of
your mortgage you can do it. You won't be the first optimistic fool to convince yourself that sunnier days and carefree ways will take the sting out of living. It's like believing
that if you move to California you'll wake up with a six-
pack and Cameron Diaz's kid sister as a girlfriend. Aren't
you missing something in that dream of yours? There'll be
someone you know tagging along. You. Which based on
your current state of mind makes your chances of contentment slim to zero.

Instead of watching with horror as forty years of *The
Office* slip by in your mind's eye, how about tuning in to
the smaller picture? You seem to have succumbed to a
depression brought on by the realisation of the fundamental
irrelevance of your one little life. Seen from a certain
vantage point you are absolutely right. It doesn't matter if
you live or die, drink lager until you burst or actively cultivate your own little crop of melanomas in the midday sun.
On the other hand, isn't that equally pointless? Giving your
current life a bad review and imagining that life in the sun
will be nothing but fun is so much easier than addressing
your problems in a sensible, constructive way. It might help
if you look a little further afield than the four corners of
your mind, flat and workplace.

I'm not blaming you for questioning the meaning of life. It's something that we could all do with scrutinising from time to time. We've created a society obsessed with the pursuit of personal happiness. A transitory state that's about as easy to grab hold of as a live eel smeared with Hawaiian Tropic. Happiness is the occasional reward you receive for living well, not a career goal that you can point your big guns at, aim and achieve.

It's a cliché, but often the less you have the more chance you have of achieving a happy state. There's a lot of clutter obscuring the path to inner contentment in our society. Without all that paraphernalia the view gets much clearer. Certainly, by default, giving it all up might afford you a glimpse of what really counts in life. But it's a risky business. The road to happiness is more likely to be under your nose than under a hot sun. I don't want to start sounding like a Pepsi ad, but have you taken a look around you recently? Watched a glorious sunset on the way home from work, seen two old people holding hands and felt your heart leap? Have all the tiny acts of human kindness that go on every day completely escaped your attention?

Only one person can make your life worth living and that's you. It may be stating the obvious but most countries offering golden beaches and the drifter lifestyle have plenty of problems of their own. The inhabitants would generally exchange a selection of limbs for the lifestyle you so disdain. It's ironic that here we are, a bunch of spoilt Westerners who want for little, all wishing we could swap lifestyles with Third World villagers. The feeling is mutual. Why do you think there's a steady stream of immigrants risking life and limb to get to this country? Do things like freedom, democracy, a health service or even public transport (such as it is) mean anything to you? They probably would if you were a twenty-six-year-old African.

I suggest that before you do anything radical you should embark on a horizon-broadening sabbatical. Establish whether the grass really is greener on the other side. How about taking a month's holiday and helping one of the many marine-conservation societies eager for skilled volunteers? My suspicion is you need to start feeling useful. Then again if it's a quick fix you're after you could pop off to your local doctor and get him to put you on Prozac – just one of the many little luxuries of First World living.

I Miss Him More in Winter

A year ago I split up with someone and still haven't got over it. I've made a real effort to get on with my life, but I still miss my ex, and sometimes feel horribly lonely. The longer nights only make it worse. I know the relationship is over – so how can I put it behind me once and for all?

You poor thing. I know exactly what you mean. The air smells of decay and hope lies discarded amongst the rotting leaves. OK, I may be over-dramatising a bit but winter's approach is hard to ignore. Summer is a fabulous time to be single. The sun brings out the hedonist in us all. Perhaps it's all that light that makes us light-headed. We're giddy with possibility and each bright morning promises new beginnings. In summer we never act our age but as the nights get longer we certainly start to feel it. This is the worst time of the year as we head to a period of permanent twilight. Disappointment, resignation and finally depression usually surface as the birds (sensibly) depart. When the air starts to sharpen and perpetual evening begins to smother us in its cloak our hearts start to feel as heavy as our coats. It's hard to stay cheerful and my advice is don't bother to try. Only imbecilic optimists and hunters go galloping towards winter with enthusiastic abandon.

In fact, during its opening act, winter makes you want to run as fast as you can in the opposite direction. I remember being impressed by the cynical marketing skills of Norwegian travel agents. In late January, pasted on every single billboard in the snow-covered train station at Oslo airport, you'll find photographs of golden beaches, lapped by turquoise oceans twinkling in the sparkling sunlight. It's almost unbearably tempting to go back into the terminal, march up to the closest airline counter and book a one-way ticket to Barbados. Even if it means sharing an island with Cliff Richard. They're probably the most effective advertisements on earth.

The first thing you have to remember is that although you're feeling lonely you are not alone. Whether you're a country or a city dweller, out there in that blanket of blackness hundreds and thousands of people just like you are fighting off their emotional demons. It's a cold time of year and I don't mean just the weather. As Christmas approaches all those artificial lights don't fool anyone. Fairy lights are the seasonal equivalent of rose-tinted glasses – only a little more desperate.

You might feel miserable but there are people out there who'd give their pension cheque for your problems. It makes me miserable just thinking about all those lonely old people, cloistered in retirement homes (or the lucky few still in their own homes), being ignored by children and grandchildren alike. Their friends are dead or dying, their spouses already departed, and yet they battle on, bravely facing up to a decreasing future. Their only certainty that they're getting one step closer to the great unknown every day. You probably think you'd like a hug. Some of these people haven't felt the touch of another human being, apart from their GPs, for years. They sit in silent living rooms over economy meals trying to make the best of the situation. Which usually involves making excuses for busy offspring who don't even have time to telephone. No, this is not a happy time of year.

The fact that you're feeling down about it marks you out as intelligent, sensitive and interesting. A woman like you doesn't stay single for long. The only thing that's keeping you from another relationship is the fiction you've created around the last one. You probably think he was the only man for you. No one understood you, loved you or cared for you like he did. Even as I write it I feel the heavy hand of cynicism strike my keyboard. For all I know he was pretty near perfect but I sincerely doubt it. He was probably a human being just like the rest of us and the odds are, apparently, that every hundredth man you meet has your name written all over him. That said, odds aren't that predictable. You might have to struggle through a year or five, shake the hands of a thousand undesirable strangers, and then suddenly you'll meet a hundred potential partners all in one night. I've never heard of it happening like that but there's always a first time.

Not that I recommend getting out there and embarking on a one-woman search party for Mr Maybe. I may veer away from popular opinion here but I'm all for indulging your misery. Savour every moment and treat it like in happier days you might cystitis. Self-medication is a must. When you're heartbroken or depressed, well-meaning friends will insist on dragging you out. All that does is drag you down. The men who didn't fancy you that night and the others that repulsed you only confirm that you are without question undatable . . . and possibly have two heads. Both of which resemble a rhino's bottom. Of course you're wrong but in that sort of mood you haven't a hope in hell of realising it.

Far better to immerse yourself in a mission to transform your bedroom into a cosy nest of comfort and luxury. If needs be, sell the rest of your furniture in order to fund fab sheets, scented candles, plump novels, a TV/video and, most importantly of all, a furry hot-water bottle or an electric blanket. Then settle yourself in for a self-indulgent and gorgeously warm winter. Squirrels aren't as stupid as we think. When you finally venture out you'll find the whole world has changed (and it might only be December).

I'm Scared of Girls

I am eighteen years old and I have a serious confidence crisis. I am doing well at college, good grades, nice career prospects – and nice family. The only problem I have involves girls, and to be more precise my confidence. Ever since I approached a girl in class and made a complete fool of myself and got rejected it has become a mounting problem for me even to talk to a girl, fearing some sort of repercussion. I really don't know what to do.

All my friends brag about their girlfriends and I feel left out of it. Girls do look at me but I don't honestly have the guts to approach them. Every time I walk towards them something inexorably pulls me back. I am seriously going crazy. I try to ignore girls and concentrate on my studies and stuff but to say my social life is dull would be an understatement. Please help.

The good news is that you're certainly on the right path now, even if it is by default. Such is the contrary nature of the opposite sex that the more you ignore them the more likely you are to have them creeping all over you like fungus. There's nothing a woman finds more attractive in a man than what appears to be utter indifference. If you were female you'd now be utterly besotted by the person who turned you down. Their rejection would serve as confirmation of their higher intellect and their acute perceptive powers. They, you would have concluded, were capable of seeing right through your presentable façade to the dull, uninspiring and downright unappealing human beneath the skin. Thanks to their unique insight into the real you they are obviously the one person marked out for you to share your life with.

Luckily for you, you're not a woman but you do nevertheless have problems. We can sort this out. You'd be surprised how many guys are in the same boat. Have you heard of the Hollywood actor Benicio Del Toro? He's en route to becoming my new guru, a philosopher genius of unparalleled profundity. Just check out this quote from a newspaper interview, which appeared recently: 'What women don't know is all a man gets from the moment he's born is rejection. So any time he gets the breath of a chance, he's going to take advantage.' Now Benicio is on a lot of women's Top Ten Totty list, he's the sort of guy you can't imagine anyone saying no to and yet here he is bleating on about the agony of rejection and using it as his excuse for a lifetime of bad behaviour.

Notwithstanding the fact that as an actor he's surely suffered the agony of rejection on a daily basis, or at least would have done until he popped that first Oscar into his display cabinet. What has some Puerto Rican thespian with an anthracite bouffant got to do with you? I use him merely as an example to illustrate how universal your problem is.

Show me a guy who doesn't feel a little trepidation about asking a girl out and I'll show you a half-wit. I have it on good authority that once the ripple of fear disappears so does the pleasure. Where's the sport in knowing you are going to get yes for an answer? One of the greatest moans from heartthrob male celebrities is the loss of the thrill of the chase. There's nothing less attractive to a man apparently than quoting him his CV while waving your already dispensed with La Perla knickers in his face. Movie stars like George Clooney, Matt Damon and Hugh Grant pray to be rejected. It's a typical case of the grass being utterly verdant on your neighbour's side of the fence.

We've established that rejection is all part of the experience. Now it's time to talk about venue. I know you've had a traumatic experience so I don't want to be too hard on you, but what were you thinking about when you decided to make your approach in a crowded classroom? A person less understanding than me would mark you out as a certifiable masochist. Were you after public humiliation? The subtlety of a college corridor too unexciting for you? A furtive locker encounter too discreet? What about email or texting, the least painful forums for rejection we've come up with yet? I suggest you seek out a little privacy next time you ask a girl out. We like our private lives to stay that way, until we get together with our girlfriends and divulge the nitty-gritty, that is.

You've suffered a minor setback and it's got you all a-quiver. You are going to need to toughen up if you want to mark out a place for yourself in this world. One person rejecting you cruelly will start to feel like foreplay when you step into the job market. Whoever it was that caused you such humiliation actually did you a huge favour. She's taught you a valuable lesson that you are still struggling to take advantage of. The way to deal with a knock is to pick yourself up, dust off your despair and kick off where you last fell. What comes easily in this world is rarely worth having.

So get on with your studies and concentrate on making friends of both sexes. Girls aren't some breed apart to be approached with caution. They're flesh and blood and full of complexes, just like you. Get to know a couple and you'll soon discover that they're not as scary as you think. Then again it depends on what you're looking for. I suggest friendship is a good place to start.

He Thinks I Love Books More Than Him

I live with my partner and our two-year-old daughter. I have always dreamt of becoming a published writer, and love to read. Since our daughter was born I find myself with less and less time, and my partner complains when I spend my precious spare time with a book, or at the typewriter, instead of being with him and our daughter. He treats my love of books as though it was an affair. Even if he's watching TV he wants me to watch it with him rather than read nearby. So many writers have partners in the business. Should I really be with someone who doesn't understand my passion for books?

I can hear sighs of recognition countrywide. I'm sure there is not a mother or parent out there who doesn't crave the downtime they used to take for granted. I'm not minimising your dilemma. It may even be far greater than it appears if your husband really has so little sympathy with your favourite pastime. I don't want this to turn into my bi-monthly bout of man-bashing. A sort of feminist Tourette's that overcomes me every now and again for no explicable reason. Then again, for the great pleasure it affords me I'm sure you guys will allow me the luxury. Embrace it as the playful teasing it's meant to be rather than as a verbal vasectomy.

For example, why is it that men find it so objectionable for their partner to forgo the delights of communing with their TV addiction? If a woman wants to watch a movie, or catch her favourite programme, she is more than happy to do it alone. Indeed the peace and quiet to watch *Friends*,

West Wing or drool over the Scud Stud remain coveted but often unrequited desires.

Whingeing away on the other side of the sexual divide is the man of the house. His plaintive complaint? 'You never do anything with me.' What he's referring to isn't the walk on Sunday you wish he'd accompany you on, or the trip to the theatre or even a football match. It's not an invitation to slip into the bath with him. Instead it refers to his desire to hold you hostage on the sofa, clamped to his side like a colostomy bag, trapped by an imprisoning forearm masquerading as affection and forced to suffer silently while he flicks through the channels before settling on some war movie you've seen ten times.

It's a long-winded way of saying don't think I don't understand! That doesn't mean there aren't two sides to this story. Maybe your books (or your relationship to them) have taken on irrationally immense proportions in both your minds. It's easy to focus on one small frustration rather than take in the full spectrum.

You sound resentful towards your husband, as though he's to blame for not being a fellow writer, editor or even reader. Perhaps you feel that it would give you the leg-up or support for your writing-career that you imagine everyone else has. I can assure you it's not the case. Maybe you just notice the writers who are lucky enough to have partners involved in a similar pursuit. Plenty don't have partners at all.

Writing tends to be a lonely, miserable and competitive business. I've got a writer friend obsessed with other novelists' ages. She visits bookstores to scan their dates of birth and confirm her worst fear that every writer in the world is half her age. Curiously she never picks up novels by septuagenarians.

Your husband's lack of literary interest is not his fault.

He hasn't given up on books in order to punish you; it sounds like they were just never his thing. That's hard to live with if they are your passion but it's certainly not uncommon. Many couples continue to enjoy separate interests, from opera to gardening, pot-holing, fishing, visiting a dominatrix, whatever. It's how much space they give each other to pursue them that's important.

Are you frustrated about your writing and taking it out on your husband? Or is he a selfish brute whose omnipresence in all aspects of your life has started to seem too high a price to pay for your marriage? If the latter is the case, start planning your exit. If not, read on.

Perhaps he senses your resentment about the loss of intellectual stimulation and doesn't know what to do except blame the messenger. In this case your increasing collection of accusingly unread books. Reading is one of life's great pleasures, if it gives you pleasure. It's also an activity that thankfully has legs, as they say. Right now you're pushed for time and fear your brain is withering. Soon enough your daughter will be grown up and you'll be left in peace with your library.

Meantime I suggest you negotiate. Tell your husband you want a fixed amount of time a week to devote to reading and offer him the likewise for his chosen pursuit. Then put your oldest books into storage to give him some space and, taking advantage of the upsurge in good will, join a book club so you can talk to like-minded people about your passion once a month.

I've Got a Teeny Weeny

I was inspired to write after I read an article about a man who'd been charged with a sex crime the other day. Not that I'm a criminal but the headline read 'Teeny Weeny' and that's what I've got. The gentleman in question had been charged and subsequently cleared of a sex attack because the victim described his penis as four inches long. The defence replied that at best, fully erect, their client could struggle to an inch and a half. Well, I'm not quite as erectily challenged as him but at best I can muster two and a half (inches, that is).

I've only had one sexual relationship in my life and during that brief period it didn't seem to matter. Now I've met a girl I really like but I'm ashamed to go to bed with her, as I'm sure I'll just disappoint her and lose her.

Two and a half inches – you lucky man. I've just read a book about an hermaphrodite whose penis was no bigger than a raisin. Actually, it's a great novel by Jeffrey Eugenides, which you might enjoy, called *Middlesex*. Not that I'm questioning your sexuality here. You sound like you're all man. But the theme of a character nervous to reveal his genitalia might have resonance with you. It takes guts to write a letter like yours in this competitive sexual climate. Everywhere you look people are having fantastic sex that is not only imaginative, satisfying and pays homage to the Marquis de Sade but goes on for four or five hours, five times a week. Pulease! Who are these people? They're like the Loch Ness monster, alive only in our imaginations and the pages of the tabloids.

One of the most sexually charged moments in cinema history is in *The Tin Drum* when a fugitive takes refuge in a muddy potato field under Oskar's grandmother's four skirts, and his mother is conceived. Or at least it's one of my favourites. The point is that sex is never simple, as anyone brave enough to voice his or her secret desires will tell you.

I recall in the eighties asking a gay friend in the light of Aids whether he still had penetrative sex. He replied that he'd never really enjoyed penetration and that gay men were continually baffled by heterosexuals' reliance on it. I was surprised. Only being familiar with the stereotype of gay sex: anal, penetrative, and if possible on Hampstead Heath. To this day I still regret not quizzing him.

I suspect that thanks to obvious challenges gay men and lesbians have a lot to teach we unimaginative heteros. The Freudian theory of a 'mature' orgasm which is vaginal rather than clitoral (and of course depends on a GIANT, manly, thrusting member to tickle your G-spot) is severely discredited these days. It's like the Holy Grail – a lovely thing, but there's little chance of coming across it. Most women will tell you that unless you're in the vicinity of their clitoris you've got no hope of making them come. A man like you has a good chance of hitting the spot.

The porn rush of the early seventies celebrated women's release from the bondage of their fertility (thanks to the pill) by introducing them to the bondage of casual sex. In these 'celebratory' flicks we were penetrated right, left and centre by a succession of enormous organs that kept their owners at arm's length, literally. They feature women groaning in pleasure as a man with a rolling pin for a penis supposedly supplies the ultimate in ecstasy. What women are actually getting is cystitis. A recent glimpse of a Swedish porn channel suggested not much had changed, apart from the facial hair. Being used as a form of stopcock is not most girls' idea of pleasure. Yet every hetero porn flick I've ever seen features the guy (or guys) looking down in a state of self-admiringly sexual nirvana as their inflated member pumps in and out of an increasingly traumatised vagina, while managing to avoid any contact at all with the woman's clitoris.

During the barbaric practice of female circumcision they don't remove the girl's clitoris by accident. By slicing off the organ that gives women sexual pleasure they are sentencing these women to a life devoid of sexual consummation. In the Western world, although it's thankfully left in place, it's often overlooked like the wallflower at a school dance.

You are in the perfect position to embark on a journey of sexual exploration that could turn you into the greatest lover on earth. You could even write a book about it: *Adventures of the Pocket-sized Penis?* Without the distraction of a personal tree trunk to flaunt in gym changing rooms and impale the nearest woman who'll let you on, you might actually discover what makes women tick. A girlfriend of mine slept with a world-famous Lothario who had women hanging off him like Christmas-tree decorations. Obviously she reported back. 'Well, was it HUGE?' we asked her. 'Surprisingly small,' she replied, but with a smug grin on her face that made the Cheshire Cat look grumpy. 'Oh . . .' we continued. 'But I had the best bloody night of sex I've ever had or will have. He made me come fifteen times and that was before we even got around to penetrative sex.'

Women misrepresented their behavioural, emotional and sexual differences from the opposite sex during post-emancipation mayhem. Now we're trying to clear up the mess. By aping men in the boardroom and the bedroom we delivered a misleading portrait of who we are and what pleasures us. The idea of the 'hot rod' thrusting home its top-priority semen-delivery is certainly not every woman's, and I suspect not any woman's, sexual fantasy. We aspire to soft lips and rough sex, sensitive fingers, lovers with an eye for atmosphere, an imagination and the inclination to experiment. An interest in what individually we find stimulating is no bad thing. And of course sometimes we just fancy a quickie in the corridor. There are no hard and fast rules but hard and fast members aren't the answer.

The one thing you can't offer much of comes low on our list of priorities. There are plenty of men out there with giant phalluses that they're all too happy to thrust at you along with their Ferrari and their black American Express card. I think they imagine that we can be impressed into climax. Any dick can muster an erection; it's what he does with it that counts.

I'm Terrified of Commitment

My boyfriend and I have been together nearly four years and he's very keen to settle down. I, however, am terrified of commitment (I have mistrusted the idea of marriage or similar ever since my parents split up when I was fourteen) and keep thinking perhaps I should finish it. What do you think?

It's not an either/or situation as far as I can see. Your unfortunate partner might be enduring the after-effects of your dysfunctional childhood but it doesn't mean you have to leave him in order to sort it out. Of course you're a commitment-phobe: Who wouldn't be after watching their parents divorce? There are an awful lot of women out there like you. It's just hard to spot them since they're all wearing the equivalent of an emotional chador. The only difference between women and men on this score is that a terror of commitment is one emotional state that men aren't afraid to admit to. Women on the other hand are suffering a sort of mass delusion, the kind you normally only find in cult sects. The thoroughly modern Ms pretends that all she wants is a stable, committed relationship and then does everything in her power to avoid it.

Whether it's because we set our sights on serial bachelors in the naive belief we can change them, or men who are way out of our league, or men who live in foreign parts or men too young to be responsible or men too old to want to start again we manage – while taking no responsibility – to ensure that we don't actually end up with what we really don't want. A mature, committed relationship. After all, these days we're spoilt for choice in much the same way as men used to be two centuries ago when seeking a bride. Do we go for the pretty, useless one, the dark, challenging one, the blond, trophy one, the bespectacled, serious one, the ambitious, arrogant one? Let's not leave it to men to do the stereotyping! When it comes to choosing a partner modern women are as confused as five-year-olds at a pic 'n mix counter. After so long without choices it's not surprising. The trouble is that like strident Zionists we don't seem to have learnt from our own bitter experience. We've adopted the qualities that in men drive us to the cliff edge in despair. Why can't we actually admit it? Women hate being called devious but in this area we are unforgivably duplicitous. Ironically it's only ourselves we're deceiving.

I watch my friends commit the same crime over and over again. Only the other day I bumped into a girlfriend in a state of high agitation. 'I've just split up with Paul,' she announced. 'What a shame,' I replied. 'He seemed so lovely.' 'He was lovely all right, so lovely he put me on a pedestal and worshipped me. Thought I was the best thing since sliced bread. Wanted to hang out with me all the time . . .' 'So what went wrong?' 'Well, nobody could be expected to take that sort of claustrophobic adulation day in day out, could they?' she exploded at me in exasperation.

I was confused. Last time I'd seen her she'd been on the verge of a nervous breakdown. The result of dating a man who wanted an 'open' relationship. She was convinced, and desperately trying to convince him, that she was the one. I remember her telling me how much they had in common; a list that included birthplace and an interest in the theatre. The fact that he was serially committed to remaining single and all she wanted was to settle down didn't diminish her enthusiasm for him as a life partner. In short she didn't accept there was a conflict. If she truly dreamt of the kind of relationship she paid lip service to why was she dating a man who ran a harem? Now here she was chucking her new man for wanting her to be his one and only. That's what I mean about commitment-phobic women. Their capacity for self-delusion is beyond delusional!

It's no wonder that a serial bachelor like George Clooney is top of every woman's fantasy list. Apart from his obvious attributes, a major aspect of his appeal to the opposite sex is that he swears blind he'll never marry again. Instead of taking him at his word women across the globe dream of changing his mind. Perhaps we just don't know how to take no for an answer, perhaps we're masochists who really enjoy banging our heads against brick walls, or perhaps we want to play the field as much as our opposite sex? We just have an honesty problem when it comes to admitting it!

You don't have to be a genius to recognise there's something wrong. If you're dating a married man with three children because you want a faithful partner to settle down and have kids with then you need help. What we're all terrified of is discovering we haven't got what it takes to make a relationship work. And we're probably right to be afraid. Most of us these days are spoilt by choice. We need to learn to lower our gaze from the horizon in the hope of something better and instead turn it to the person in front of our noses. So he's not the handsome, rich, gorgeous, attentive, difficult, easy-going, loving, exciting, well-endowed, passionate, complicated, simple man we dreamed we'd end up with. He might only embody a couple of those qualities, but there's one important difference. He's real, he's there and he's ready to love us back. That makes up for an awful lot. You're already a giant leap ahead. Take a long hard look at your man. I suspect that if you remove your rose-tinted binoculars you might find that what you're really after is right in front of your nose.

My In-laws Want My Husband's Sperm

My problem is a thorny one. My brother-in-law and his wife can't have children, and need a sperm donor. Since my brother-in-law can't have children he's asked my husband – the next best thing, I suppose – to donate sperm. My husband feels he'd like to do this, but the whole situation makes me *very* apprehensive. Am I being selfish?

Yikes, hand me my crystal ball and big hoop earrings. Seriously, I wouldn't like to be in your shoes. I'm not even sure I'm qualified to answer your dilemma but I'll have a dig. One thing I'm pretty confident of is that you're not acting jealously or selfishly. I don't want to come to premature conclusions but I suspect if there is any selfish behaviour it's emanating from the direction of your in-laws. Frankly I don't blame you for casting your net far and wide in an attempt to find answers. Emotional responses are as unpredictable as they can be devastating. This is an emotional minefield and even I'm terrified to put my foot in it.

Your brother-in-law may be suffering a sense of entitlement. It's a condition we all seem to be experiencing to some extent these days. Women remembering to have kids at forty, gay and lesbian couples who don't see why their sexual orientation should preclude them having children, the biologically incapable looking to science for small miracles. Your brother-in-law needs to wake up and face the facts. Whoever the donor is the baby will not be 'his' in purely genetic terms. Big deal, some might say. The gift of a child is enough to render 'the making of' irrelevant. For others, procreation is solely about 'mirroring'. You can spot them a mile off holding a crimson, bawling bundle of newborn and insisting it's got their eyes.

Perhaps your brother-in-law's sperm is just napping? A friend of mine was recently going through a torpid phase that happened to coincide with his taking a fertility test. One look at his sample and the doctor pronounced it dormant. Not dead but in a wilful state of suppression. Happily, my friend's mood changed and a week later he was delighted to report that not only was his sperm active again but also it was apparently 'superior'. To celebrate, he generously offered us all (his female friends) the opportunity of visiting the clinic and trying it out for ourselves. Perhaps you should relay this happy tale to your brother-in-law and get him to check again?

You say (in your unabridged letter) you are becoming broody. It's a useful word that suggests a longing, out of your control, peculiarly female and certainly not your responsibility. Could this be a pelvic reaction to your brother's request? Had you given motherhood a thought until he started wanting your husband's sperm? The last thing you need to do is rush into having a child you're not ready for. On the other hand perhaps you are ready? You don't say what your husband feels but I'm presuming he's not averse to parenthood. It would certainly be an easy way out of your current dilemma. 'Sorry, love to help and all that but there's only so much sperm to go around and we're currently employing our quota in pursuit of our own little procreative act.' Your brother-in-law can hardly expect his sibling to choose in his favour, rather than his wife's.

Then again the idea of two little kids, the closest of cousins, growing up in separate but intimately connected households isn't so awful. We manage to squeeze exes and stepchildren, illegitimate surprises, recently unearthed parents, adopted children, siblings the same age as our offspring, fifth wives, long-lost lovers and so many more into the broader church of what today constitutes family. Is it so bad that this brother wants a little bit of your husband with which to make a slightly complicated nephew?

The real focus must be on timing. Had you already been pregnant when your brother-in-law made his request you might have looked on it more kindly. You'd certainly feel less proprietorial about your spouse's sperm. It's a woman thing. Once we've got the It Gucci coat we don't care who else buys one. Until we possess it we're locked in mortal combat with the rest of the country's fashionistas. I'm sure the sperm battle is based on equally base instincts. This is not to minimalise your feelings, merely to drag them from the relative safety of your own brain into the harsh light of scrutiny!

Congratulations, by the way – your husband sounds like a nice guy. Not many men would be as happy to oblige their sibling's request. You probably wish he was more like most of them. But actually that big heart is probably what you married him for in the first place. The most important relationship to consider is not that of the two siblings (who will always remain brothers) or the unborn child (who may never materialise). Your brother-in-law can always get his sperm off the shelf. A shelf that if you two don't work out what your relationship can withstand you might find yourselves back on!

Nobody has a divine right to parenthood or selection and that includes you and your brother-in-law. Discuss the possibilities and make a *joint* decision based on the considered outcome. And good luck.

After Eight Years My Lover's Still Married

I have been with a man for eight years, whom I love very much, and we have a one-year-old daughter together. The problem is that he is married. He doesn't love his wife, who he says is an unkind, unloving person – but feels he must stay with her until their teenage children leave home. No one knows he is my child's father as he has begged me to keep it a secret. When I became pregnant he was thrilled, much to my surprise, and said that he would support us financially. But he hasn't given me a penny and I'm starting to wonder if he's ever going to leave his wife. I want to trust him, but I'm not sure if I can any more.

I wish I could tell you that yours is an unusual or original story. Unfortunately it's not. Instead your situation is a tragic but predictable example of what happens to all but the very lucky few who embark on an affair. Decent people move on from unsatisfactory relationships before forming new ones. Weak people cheat on their partners. I'm constantly surprised at how many people are prepared to begin a relationship founded on lies and expect it to flourish. I know that love can be blind but eight years is a long time to spend stumbling around in the dark.

Perhaps you've come to the wrong person. I've never understood how we can expect fidelity and a committed relationship from someone who has already broken that promise to somebody else. The whole world apparently has issues of low self-esteem but in this one scenario we become arrogant beyond belief. You are in a wholly unenviable and totally escapable position. This man has taken far too much of your time and emotional energy.

You say you love him but I think you've forgotten what love should be. Real love comes calling on the wings of respect. You surely can't respect the weak and pathetic way he has behaved towards the two women in his life for almost a decade? I mention two of you because it's easy to forget the misery he's causing his wife. You only have his word for her failings. I'm sure given air time she could equally illuminate you on a few of his shortcomings.

It's curious that in a situation like this it's never the protagonist who gets the blame. He blames his wife, she blames you, and he comes up smelling of roses. If it weren't so laughable it would be tragic.

For heaven's sake, you only have one life and you deserve better. You already have the only thing you're going to get out of this relationship and that's your daughter. Thank your lucky stars for her appearance in the world and move on. Children learn patterns of behaviour from their parents. Do you really want your daughter to end up making the same mistakes as you? Get on with teaching her to have the self-respect not to take second best in life. You don't want her falling into the same trap as you have and there is still time for both of you to make good out of bad.

First of all you must stop protecting your lover's identity. He has betrayed your trust and confidence too many times to be allowed the privilege of anonymity. I say this not in order for you to avenge yourself by exposing him but so that you can take control of your life and the situation you find yourself in. Everyone makes mistakes and keeping yours a secret only makes it appear shameful. So you've wasted too much time on a complete loser. The way to make up for it is to move on fast.

I suspect you feel like you've been kept in a holding

pattern for the duration of this relationship. You're like one of those aeroplanes endlessly circling the airport but never being allowed to land. Your every move and decision dependent on the whim of another. It's time for you to take over the controls. He's proved he can't be trusted. Of course he should be supporting his daughter. Now it's your responsibility to make sure he does. Why should she suffer in penury for your misplaced devotion? The fact that he is not paying his share should provide a clear illustration to you of what a pathetic, irresponsible man he is. You say you were surprised that he was enthusiastic about your pregnancy. I'm not surprised at all. If a person takes no responsibility for their actions, no action ever results in responsibility. It's easy for him to say have the baby when the arrival of a new life has so little impact on his own.

This has got to stop. Tell your parents, tell your friends, make a clean breast of things. You are a competent, responsible woman who has coped with and survived an incredibly difficult relationship. He is an emotional cripple. Pity him if you must but save your love for those who deserve it. Your daughter, your parents, your friends and the man who will come along and love you like you deserve. You need to cut the ties that bind you to this fool for ever. You've already made it through the darkest days. The future will be brighter by far. Write and let me know so I can say I told you so.

I Can't Cope with Being HIV-positive

I am HIV-positive. I live on the Cornish coast and I try to stay healthy by taking my drugs and swimming every day. I still enjoy a good flirt; only the other night a guy pinched my bum at a bar, and I've even managed to forgive the person I contracted the disease from. However, most days I still feel soiled, dirty, furious with the world and unable to cope. I know there are people with worse problems than mine, it's just hard to think what they might be. I'm tempted to give up the drugs and let fate takes its course. Am I being pathetic or have I endured more than my fair share?

There's no denying that you've endured more than your fair share of misery. But what is a fair share? As you so nobly point out, even in your disadvantaged position there are people out there worse off. I certainly don't need to lecture you on living with HIV but like most people I have friends who are healthy and active despite being infected. From the minimal detail in your unabridged letter it sounds like most of the time you are one of them. You describe swimming daily and flirting regularly. You even have complete strangers pinching your bum. You should count yourself lucky. That hasn't happened to me since I visited Rome for the first time in my teens! Perhaps I'll pop down to Cornwall one of these weekends.

As you can see I have had to edit your long letter and attempt to extract the essence. I hope you will forgive me and that I have done you justice. It may seem like a cruel irony that your 'dilemma' is included in an issue on ageing. I thought it might appeal to your sense of humour to find yourself nestling among people fretting about sagging, bagging and wrinkling. Conditions which I'm sure you would swap your illness for any day. Without wanting to sound like an over-zealous missionary it also seemed a good time to remind the healthy of a few pertinent facts. While we're worrying about the trivial problems that come with advancing years there are people out there with far greater concerns.

Isn't that the thing about human beings? No sooner do we sympathise with one person's problems then along comes someone suffering even harsher woes. I wish you could see all the letters I receive. Perhaps I'll send you a bundle. I really do think they might cheer you up. I remember once being in a state of deep depression, over some man or other, until my best friend turned up to comfort me. She promptly burst into tears and started to tell me about the miseries she was going through. Not to sound selfish or anything but her problems went a long way to making me feel better. I wouldn't have swapped places with her for a second!

We humans really are a sensitive bunch. Broken hearts, betrayal, illness, abuse, poverty, it's easy to wonder at times why we bother going on. The only answer I can give you is why the hell not. What are the options? You are clearly a tough, sensitive, intelligent man. Since when was nothing (which is where you'd be headed if you stopped taking the drugs) better than something? Being single and HIV-positive is miserable but so is being single with a sore throat. I'm not mocking your illness but merely pointing out that you might be confusing your issues here.

You wrote to me because you felt a real empathy with the woman dreading another winter alone. It's terrible to be dependent on drugs and miserable to have lost people you care about. But there are other people out there you have yet to meet and plenty of reasons for being alive.

Smelling the sea air of a morning on your daily swim must be pretty invigorating. It sounds like you have quite a bit of time on your hands. It also sounds like you've experienced and surmounted a series of enormous personal challenges. How about you share your secrets of survival with others fighting personal catastrophe? It might do you good and remind you that the finger of fate wasn't pointing directly at you but just waving in your general direction when you contracted the disease. You say that the burden and stigma are hard to bear and I believe you. Nevertheless twenty years ago it was a lot worse. How can you think about ending your life when half the world's Aids sufferers don't even have access to the medicine you loathe?

Personal misfortune makes us more sensitive to other people's sadness and pain. It's an all-important part of the maturing process. You've displayed an astonishing depth of character by forgiving the man who selfishly allowed you to contract the disease. What a great thing it would be if you could take that impressive sense of forgiveness, along with your unique understanding of depression and loss, and use it to help other sufferers. You have endured so much and survived. You should be proud of yourself. Isn't the obvious choice to go out and use that experience for good? Sitting around and trying to work out if the load you bear is heavier than the man's walking past your window may pass the time but it won't make you feel any better. Get up, get out and show the world what you're still capable of instead of sitting at home and admiring your wounds. People need you, don't forget it.

Must I Choose Between
My Partner and My Son?

I was divorced five years ago, and my ex-husband and I share custody of our son. I am very much in love with my current partner, and would like to settle down and have more children with him. But he has decided he needs a change of location and wants to move to Sicily – having been disillusioned with life here for some time. My husband refuses to let me take my son and I'm being forced to choose between my partner and my boy. How can I resolve this?

The easy answer and possibly the right one is that you should stay with your child. He has already been through the upheaval of your divorce and now you are considering putting him through an even more traumatic separation. You made a decision to create a little 'mini-me' and he needs you. No stepmother, however devoted, can replace you. Parenting isn't something you can resign from or pass on to someone else (except in the most extreme circumstances).

The fact that your partner is disillusioned hardly counts as a crisis. Perhaps if he had a child of his own he would comprehend the impossible situation he is putting you in? Too often in these easy-come, easy-go days people put the same degree of thought into having a child as they do into buying a puppy. I'm not suggesting you are one of them. You are obviously going through serious agonies as you try to make the right choice.

As I'm sure you're well aware, whatever you decide to do will involve a loss. Your first responsibility must lie with the life you've created. They don't call them 'form-ative' years for nothing. Then again, an unhappy parent makes for an unhappy child and if you are sitting around lovesick and miserable it won't be very good for your relationship. Have you discussed the situation with your son? You haven't told me what age he is, which makes advising you even harder. So much depends on his state of mind and stage of development. A secure teenager might think that having a second life to dip into in another country was a dream opportunity. You might even be considered to be increasing his opportunities. He could learn a new language, have his heart broken by olive-skinned temptresses with exotic names like Valéria and Marina, and have a year-round tan. Then again if he's a youngster only beginning to adjust to the complications of having two homes in one country you can hardly put him through it again.

Life, as you so rightly state, is not straightforward. There are other issues here that need addressing before you can come to any reasonable conclusion. I'm interested to note that you describe this as a choice between your partner and your son. There's no suggestion that your partner is open to an alternative. In fact that's what worries me most about the whole business. It feels like you are being forced to choose and my first question has to be why, knowing that you have an impossible decision to make, your partner rates his happiness so much higher than yours; and more importantly your child's.

A compromise or a delay would seem to be the reason-able course of action. Instead it sounds like he's already packed his bags for his new life and won't countenance anything other than your doing likewise. I'm not suggesting you give him up, but could this relationship be more complicated than you are giving it credit? He's hardly reciprocating your devotion by forcing you to make such a choice. In fact it seems bloody selfish. Your little boy won't be a child for ever. What's the harm in waiting a little while for your sunny idyll?

Quite possibly the answers to your partner's problems may not even lie in the move to another country. Disillusionment is a state of mind, not based on geographical location. Could it be that he's trying to assuage his own pain by inflicting pain on you? Or that he's feeling insecure and by forcing you to make this choice he thinks he'll get confirmation of your affection? I'm not suggesting malice in his motives but causing pain to those closest to us is an all too common response to our own internal agony. In times of darkness our natural inclination is to grope for the light. Your partner may be taking it too literally! I'm sure that in sunny Italy there are people who wake up miserable too.

Am I Addicted to Love?

I've passed my fiftieth and after two failed marriages I remain alone, searching for love, companionship and a healthy sex life. I'm worried that I am addicted to love. I just can't seem to find that special woman and so I keep searching. It does mean doing a lot of sampling. The other day I was told that I am in denial of my dominant-male instincts. All I know is that I miss the warmth of another human being beside me and sometimes I feel very lonely. Am I an old goat, in denial of my base instincts, or just another human being looking for lasting love?

The only thing you're in denial of is being at heart a human being. It's rare to find a person who admits to being lonely and actively desiring a partner. In this tough dog-eat-dog world it's not acceptable to acknowledge a craving for the warmth of your fellow man or woman. Yet do we not spend our entire lives seeking out other humans for company and comfort? People spend fortunes on massage and facials and therapies, most of which are merely imaginative (and lucrative) ways for others to use our desire for the attentive touch of another person as a business opportunity. You describe the textbook terrors of the broken-hearted but it appears that you think you're unique and perhaps a little depraved as a result of your longing. Desiring sex and seeking out potential lovers is instinctive; convincing yourself that any of this is anything but normal is what needs scrutinising. Judging by your letter I can't help feeling you've been devouring a gluttonous amount of self-help books or seeing a shrink with a bad vocabulary.

Denial this, denial that, addicted to love, suffused with dominant-male instincts . . . If you don't mind me saying so, you sound great. What's wrong with all that stuff? Or is it that you don't want everyone to know that you're human?

I can understand you being paranoid. This addicted-to-love business is getting out of control. Only the other day I nearly choked on my stuffed olive when a virtual stranger at a drinks party 'came clean' about his 'love addiction'. 'I'd ask you out but I've been told I mustn't.' 'I'd come if you weren't insane and I wasn't married,' I felt like replying. And there I was thinking he was flirting with me because he found me attractive. Perhaps I'm the one in denial, but aren't we all crazy about love? It's a condition that has plundered mental illness for its descriptive power since time immemorial, or at least 1965. I'm crazy for you, you're driving me insane, I'm madly in love, she's bonkers about him. It's not hot-off-the-press, hold-the-front-page news that love makes us act mental, or should that be mentally challenged? Cupid's arrow has been making fools of us for centuries. Since when did we have to be diagnosed for it?

I shudder when I think of all those people shipping themselves off to clinics where the greatest insanity is the prices they charge. Fully fledged adults shuffling down corridors wearing humiliating signs saying 'Love Addict' or 'Sex Addict' or 'Hoovering Addict'. Didn't we fight a world war so people didn't have to humiliate themselves by wearing signs? Now we're not only volunteering but also paying for the privilege. 'Phone Addict' I could just about understand as a potential threat to one's health, even if the danger comes from fellow pedestrians driven to peaks of rage by the cacophony of one-sided conversations deafening them on a daily basis. You just need to walk down any high street and you can't fail to notice our addiction to communication. But sex addict, love addict, food addict – talk about oversimplification. It strikes me as nothing more than a genius way to give people a condition so they'll return for treatment time and time again.

If you fall in love intermittently throughout your life, are you a love addict, a difficult person or a lucky bastard? What does love addict mean, for Christsakes? Is there one of us who can stand up and say we're not looking for love unless we've found it? 'No, I'm not looking for love, I'm looking for a spot of malice, actually. Got any?' If you're not interested in love and sex you're in denial, or as the lengthier Ethiopian saying goes, 'As a baboon can't see its red bottom so a human being can't see their own shortcomings.' Anyway, sorry, this time I really have gone off on a tangent.

Of course there are people out there for whom sex represents love withheld and therefore they can't get enough of it, or love represents future sex so they can't get enough of it, or phone sex makes them think of their grandmothers. We've all got problems and dilemmas, some of us from time to time will need professional help, but can we please stop being so bloody literal. As for you, sir: there's nothing wrong with you. Just try and choose a little more carefully in future when it comes to prospective partners and let your libido know who's boss.

My Friend Is a Gossip

I have a problem with a girlfriend and I'm not sure what to do about it. We have known each other for about six years and we became much closer recently after my father died and she was very supportive. The trouble is I think she's a gossip. In the last six months other people have repeated to me three very personal things I told her. I don't want to cause a fuss but I'm sure she's responsible as in two of the instances no one else knew about it apart from her. It's difficult because I really like her and I don't want to get into a fight. I suppose my question is how do you sustain a friendship with someone you don't trust?

The short answer is you can't. I sometimes think that the word 'friend' has become desperately undervalued in recent times. It's a bit like 'pension', which suggests security and trustworthiness, a distant halcyon future, but actually it's not worth the sum of its three syllables, let alone relying on for your retirement when it comes down to it. Ever since kissing became an acceptable form of greeting we seem to have become confused about the meaning of friendship. Perhaps we're just not used to getting so physical with strangers. In the old days a handshake kept casual acquaintances at arm's length. Nowadays lips pucker for almost anyone, from the babysitter to the gynaecologist. Since we're not naturally a touchy-feely race, once we've done saliva, lips to cheek, perhaps we mistake it as a sign of real friendship?

Confusion reigns over how we define a friend. Is it someone we can share a joke with? A person in whose company we like to have a drink? Someone who goes to the same gym? Has children at the same school? A colleague at work who we occasionally socialise with? Or should the term be reserved for those we can trust with our deepest fears, our stupidest indiscretions, and alone in a house with our beloved with no fear of betrayal? A friend should never be someone who waves our secrets around like a plate of hors d'oeuvres for anyone who fancies a tidbit. Why waste time on a person with whom we need to measure our revelations, hold back on the big news, modify the details, in order to prevent our most personal experiences being shared with strangers?

I admit it's hard to keep track of what 'intimate' and 'private' mean in a world where on receipt of the cheque most people are happy to invite the general public and the press's cameras to capture their 'lovely homes', to record their children's christenings, marriages, holidays and their recovery from everything from cancer to a car accident. Ironically to be invited to do so is perceived as a compliment, or increasingly 'payback' for humiliating yourself and those closest to you on some reality TV show or other.

The very ingredient that sets friendship apart from less weighty human connections is trust. Without it a friend is just a gossiping acquaintance. The sort of person Tippex was designed for. Over dinner the other night I was told the sad story of a girl whose best friend had eloped with her fiancé. Before you ask, no names were given. The discussion became animated when a male member of the gathering suggested it wasn't the absconding ex who had committed the worst act of betrayal, it was the friend. Well, being women, we turned on him like a pack of rabid dogs and snarled that it was typical of the opposite sex to dodge the responsibility. Later, thinking about it on the way home, I decided he had a point. The errant betrothed had merely followed his libido elsewhere and since when did we ever trust a libido? The friend on the other hand had performed a conscious, callous act of betrayal. It's the worst form of insider trading, stealing from a friend. And what of her profit? She lost her best friend and gained an affair. A pretty bad deal if you think about it.

To be betrayed by a lover is par for the course. It happens to all but the luckiest of us at some time or other. To be betrayed by a friend is a blow from which it's much harder to recover. Romantic liaisons are irrational by their very nature; friendship on the other hand is one of the most rational choices we make. It's a relationship made solid through shared experiences, secrets divulged, crises overcome. It's redundant when it turns into a sieve. A friend should be the person you're still talking to several divorces down the line, not the person who answers the phone when you call your ex.

Friends are the bricks we use to build a solid wall that protects us from the cruelties of the outside world. A friend you can't trust is your worst enemy. These days it's an undervalued relationship. It's deemed acceptable to break confidences and then call the victim later to see if they want a curry. What lucky people we must be to dismiss friendship so lightly. To have such great faith in the bounty of the universe that we can afford to treat those who cushion our emotional falls with so much contempt. As for what you should do, what's preferable: a short fight for the truth or a lifetime of mistrust?

Why Do You Hate Men?

Why are you so fucking sexist? Why must you always have some pathetic little dig at men? I have some advice for you. Shut up and grow up.

Haven't you heard . . . men are all the same – they just have different faces, so that you can tell them apart. What do you do if your boyfriend walks out? You shut the door. Don't imagine you can change a man . . . unless he's wearing nappies. Oops, sorry, I guess I've got the wrong guy!

Perhaps you could give me some tips on how to grow up? I do normally look to my men friends for advice on emotional maturity. Only the other day I was chatting away to . . . well, let's call him Fred. He was telling me that he's got himself into a bit of a mess. You see, he's been living with Shirley for ten years. She's actually more of a mother figure than a girlfriend. She looks after their day-to-day lives. Gets him back into line after he's been on a binge and generally makes his life a lot easier. Did I forget to mention that she's thirty-nine and has refused to have kids with him until he grows up a bit? He's a couple of years younger.

Well, Fred is just crazy about Shirley, but he's been having sex with Leslie and now Leslie's pregnant. Fred can't believe that Leslie wants to have the baby. It's going to be the final straw with Shirley – he knows that. How on earth is he going to tell her? She'll go mental and she'll probably leave him. That would be awful because he's not sure he wants to split up with Shirley. Maybe he'll just emigrate to Australia and let them fight it out between them? After all

he doesn't want kids anyway. He's way too young. Yes, he does feel a bit guilty about Shirley's biological clock – but we have to remember it's her clock, not his. His clock is telling him he must get to the West End by 8 p.m. to meet Graham.

Now Graham, he's a lovely guy. He met this wonderful girl and went from being a lascivious bachelor (his words) to a father in the space of ten months. His girlfriend Clare travels a lot because of work. He's mad about her and even crazier about his little girl who he takes care of in her absence. So what that he's carried on seeing three of his exes? He can't be expected to change completely overnight, now can he? His daughter is six.

Funny, you just reminded me of Alfie. He was sixty-three when he met Jane. Initially theirs was a professional encounter but the relationship blossomed into love. Jane, already in her late-fifties, couldn't believe her luck. They started to look for a home in Cornwall together. Actually it was Jane who started looking. The curious thing was that every time she found somewhere suitable Alfie found something wrong with it. It was starting to get a little tiresome. Also as they moved into the second year of their relationship he was still living above his office in Bloomsbury and didn't have a home phone. Meanwhile she was commuting from Hampshire to see him whenever he was free and travelling to Cornwall every time the estate agents came up with something to view. Well, guess what? It turned out that Alfie had not one but two other families on the go. All of whom had remained blissfully unaware of each other's existence until Jane stumbled upon them.

And finally there was Gerald. His wife discovered after he died of a heart attack that he'd run into financial difficulties, mortgaged their home to the hilt, failed to pay his life-insurance instalments and left her with three youngish kids to bring up on nothing. She didn't mind so much about losing the house; that was a challenge she could rise to. What troubled her was the feeling of failure. Knowing that he had gone through the entire crisis alone, never once turning to the woman who was supposed to be his partner. Whenever she'd asked him what was wrong he just used to say he was tired. Following his premature death she became insomniac with guilt. She felt a failure as a wife. On dark days believed she had as good as killed him. The truth was that Gerald had never liked talking about things and was obsessed with the possibility of failure.

I'm afraid I could carry on in this vein for quite some time. I won't. It may come as a surprise to you, but I actually love men. I count a number of them among my closest friends. That doesn't mean that I believe for a second that they're as tough, competent, emotionally secure, fearless, financially astute, good at driving, honest, lacking in vanity, or as well-adjusted as they like to make out. The trouble is that men let other men get away with murder. You need to instruct the bad apples that enough is enough. Part of it is down to lack of communication. Often it's a guy's male friends who are most shocked to discover he's a manic depressive, an alcoholic, an adulterer, was beaten by his father or is about to go bankrupt.

A guy I know had a friend who would always ask him who he was 'lashing'. It took my friend twelve years to reply, 'Well, actually, I'm more your touchy-feely kind of guy.' Men don't communicate. No wonder, when most of them are raised to put a brave face on calamity, bury their feelings and ride roughshod through the world. Men might find it hard to talk to women but in my experience they find it even harder to talk to men.

Guys. Just take a look at yourselves. You're brave enough to sacrifice yourselves for love, or country, or your children, or your football team, but you haven't got the courage to tell the woman beside you what you're feeling. Instead you've drawn battle lines between us. I bet most of you can't even remember why they're there. There seems to have been a terrible misunderstanding. When we said we wanted equal rights it wasn't a challenge; just a request for parity. We weren't saying you weren't capable of running the world any longer, just that we'd like to participate. It wasn't a battle to the last but a democratic way forward we were hoping for. We want to be friends. We want to understand you and share responsibility and do our bit to make our sex lives more satisfying. The problem is if you won't talk, how can we hear you?

My Boyfriend's a Sex-boaster

I met a lovely man through a friend a few months ago. He invited me to dinner, we got on very well, and I slept with him on that first date. We went out a few times, and everything seemed to be going well. But then during one rather drunken night in a bar he started telling me about the fabulous sex he'd had with various women in the past year – including a couple in the time we'd been going out together, complete with lurid detail. I was angry and upset and went home. He says I overreacted and is waiting for me to see sense. Apart from that one episode things were great between us. Did I overreact?

Pardon me for coming on strong, but what a jerk! This idiot you've been dating thinks he's clever because he can get laid. It's a boast that's barely worth the breath used to utter it. Nowadays sex is as easy to find as the name Smith in the phone book. The sexy thing to do is to be seen to avoid it. What you should be wondering is why it's taken you so long to see through his smarmy exterior to the serial seducer within. And if the word seducer carries any poetic resonance for you then it's time to work out why. In your (necessarily abridged) letter you say you two don't yet have 'a committed relationship'. Why on earth would you want one with this out-of-date Casanova? He's as unfashionable as those Juicy tracksuits that everyone was wearing last year.

There was a time when the world admired a 'bounder'. In Victorian days when the flicker of an eyelash was considered coming on too strong, the notion that there were people out there breaking down sexual taboos was actually quite impressive. In an era famous for its explorers these men were pioneers in their chosen field. Taking brave steps for mankind into unmapped erogenous zones in pursuit of emancipation for both sexes. In retrospect they could be viewed as pioneers, in a sexual desert, fighting for our basic human right to claim our bodies and do what we like with them. 'Bachelor' was a label to be admired, signifying a man who wasn't prepared to compromise his principles for the sake of social mores. Plenty of women would doubtless have liked to join those ranks, and indeed a brave minority did, but theirs was much more challenging terrain. To this day there's a stigma attached to being a single sexually active woman. Men are only just beginning to experience something similar.

In the twenty-first century one of the greatest day-to-day challenges for those of us in the 'free' West is escaping sex. Whether it's in movies, down the line, via the Internet, in a magazine, or in your own bed, the sheer abundance of it is enough to turn us all into sexual bulimics. I'm surprised there aren't posters that read 'Just say no'. I'm not suggesting we all take a vow of celibacy, but honestly, where's the challenge in getting your leg over? Finding love hasn't become any easier, in fact far from it, but if you're prepared to compromise, pay, or just put out, any idiot can pick up a lover.

For those reasons alone this man of yours looks tawdry. He's not mature enough to have a serious relationship so he tries to disguise his inadequacy with an abundance of 'conquests'. He obviously zooms in on long-distance lovers as the perfect way to keep things casual, and when he feels he's getting out of his depth exposes himself for the duplicitous weakling he is. This is a double-pronged attack that avoids any real action from him and also winds up the affair, or worse, extends it on his terms.

He's played you like Yehudi Menuhin does the violin. In an expert move he's left you feeling a little guilty for being unreasonable but unenthusiastic about a return to the status quo. Now he's hoping your lack of self-esteem will deliver you back to him, bullied out of having reasonable expectations and hating yourself for being weak enough to accept it. If you go back he'll have you exactly where he wants you, at arm's length to toy with as he pleases. Don't give him that opportunity.

Shakespeare's *The Taming of the Shrew* might offer you an insight into his tactics. There's no downside: if you regret dispensing with him you'll find another volunteer just around the corner. Believe me, guys like him actually do grow on trees. Then again, maybe he was just trying to impress you!

Will We Survive a Summer Apart?

My boyfriend and I are in our second year at university. He wants to spend this summer travelling as he feels he may not get the chance again. He has asked me to go with him but I've got a couple of friends getting married (I'm bridesmaid to one of them) and I want to visit my parents, who live Sweden. I've invited him to join me there for a month but his idea of hell is four weeks with me and my family! The trouble is I'm worried about what a ten-week break will do to our relationship. Should I drop my plans and follow him or stick to them and just make sure we speak a lot on the phone? I've suggested he keep a diary so I can be involved in his trip even if I can't make it.

I suggest, my dear, that you butt out. You've made your decision, now let him get on with his vacation. There is nothing more likely to create resentment and drive a rift between you both than unreasonable demands for access to his adventures. I realise that communications have greatly improved since my youth. When I was your age four weeks in Greece might as well have been four weeks in a Siberian gulag for the one left behind. Complete silence from the travelling party. It was always too hot, too early, too late, too busy or just too much bother to rustle up the drachmas and queue for an overseas call. The promise to ring would linger like an irritating chore on the otherwise sunkissed horizon. It wasn't that you didn't care, it was just that contacting home brought reality creeping into the picture. The very thing you were paying to escape.

That doesn't mean a pants-down licence to licentiousness.

Some people are quite easy-going about infidelity. I wouldn't go so far as to recommend it. A relationship needs some boundaries. Just because we live in a society where everything we want is at our fingertips doesn't mean it's good for us to have it whenever we want it. This definitely applies to sex. If you and your partner are serious about each other then I suggest you make a pact to enjoy freedom from every normal partnership responsibility, bar fidelity. If anything does happen, which even with the best intentions it might, my advice is don't admit it or discuss it when you are reunited unless you're planning to move on.

I had a letter recently from a man who was jealous of a one-night stand his girlfriend had admitted to prior to their relationship. Why she choose to enlighten him on it remains a mystery. I suspect it wasn't just for magnanimous reasons. Generally the injured party is the last person we're thinking about when we decide to come clean. Usually it's just a selfish urge to absolve ourselves of the guilt. I realise I'm bordering on the controversial here but if it's unimportant why torture your partner with unnecessary detail. That said, what I hope you'll manage, if you are committed to each other, is a couple of months that are as free of sex as they are rich in experience.

You haven't mentioned where he's planning to travel to. It does make a difference. May I make a couple of suggestions? While I'm all for giving him some rope, certain destinations are absolutely out: they include Cambodia, Vietnam and Thailand . . . you know what, make that the whole Far East. Those women are just too attractive to say no to. On the other hand he should be actively encouraged to visit anthropologically fascinating spots like Peru, Mongolia and Papua New Guinea. I once stayed at a dive resort in the latter staffed by two ex-beauty queens. When they told me they were former Miss New Guineas I dropped my scuba tank on my big toe in shock and bit through my lip to suppress a snort of laughter. For starters they were both just over four feet tall. Cultural diversity is a wonderful thing. They should have been given an award for bravery when they paraded next to the likes of Miss Brazil and Miss Sweden!

Most of Europe is a definite no no, with France being a particular hotbed of temptation. British men's pants fall off by remote control when they hear the word '*bonjour*'. If he insists, then Turkey, Albania and Croatia might be safe enough. Last time I visited the Croatian coast the fashion was for female moustaches. Although that was almost two decades ago and I believe they now import Immac.

So tell him he'll be fascinated by the volcanoes and villagers in Papua New Guinea or the history of the Dalmatian coastal town of Split. Then forget about him for a few weeks and concentrate on friends and family. Pining is banned, whether it's for the fjords or your boyfriend. If he's worth caring about he'll be back. If he isn't it's better to find out sooner rather than later. It's the sort of revelation that in your twenties provokes a couple of days of tears, in your forties a nervous breakdown.

You're young, carefree and the summer is just beginning. Enjoy yourself. Forget the diary and don't insist on phone calls or emails. If my experience with men is anything to go by that guarantees you'll be inundated!

I'm Trapped Between My Warring Parents

My parents were married for more than thirty years, but separated because my father had an affair. This had been going on for many years, but my mother never suspected until she caught them together a couple of years ago. My father and the woman are still very much together. I secretly went to see them – my mother is still very upset and certainly wouldn't want me to – and he is clearly very happy with her. It seems wrong to lie to my mother about this, but neither do I want to lose touch with my father. I feel torn between them. What should I do?

There are so many sides to this story that coming up with something as clear as the 'right' decision is virtually impossible. These days with one in two marriages ending in divorce the one thing your parents' situation is not is unique. It's surprising, or perhaps just an admirable example of the strength of human optimism, that the mere 50/50 chance that any marriage has of surviving doesn't seem to have had much impact on the expectation of the participants. It would be nice to think that in the face of grim reality, when love dies, the initially eager participants are sanguine about its demise. I've yet to come across a relationship that ended with both partners satisfied with the outcome. It's like being an Arsenal fan. Any result other than winning and you're convinced you've been robbed.

As far as winners go, it sounds like your father can count himself among them. It's a shame it took him so long to make up his mind. It's left your mother feeling betrayed and humiliated, an unavoidable situation exacerbated by the length and extent of his deception. Your father has behaved like a coward by failing to take responsibility for his actions for many years. At worst that makes him a selfish, self-serving philanderer. The far more likely scenario is that he tried his best to do the 'right thing' by all concerned and ended up in the terrible mess that dishonesty invariably creates. I suspect he wanted to keep his family together and avoid breaking your mother's heart. Unfortunately he's managed neither.

Any regular reader of this column will know that I have little time for adulterers; deceit is never a healthy option. In most cases the emotional cost increases in proportion to the length of time the dishonesty has been practised. I'm sure your mother considers it an unforgivable betrayal as much for its duration as for its existence. We all know that falling out of love is not a crime but when it happens to us we tend to treat it like one. Continuing recriminations and blame are a waste of energy and only serve to grind the shattered remains of the relationship to dust.

If you haven't been beaten, taken financial advantage of or left homeless and destitute, then painful though it is, all that's left to do is to pick yourself up and get on with life. The longer your mother acts the victim, the longer she'll be a victim. She can't expect her children to wreak revenge for their father's infidelity. Heartbreak takes time to recover from but when an abandoned lover wilfully prolongs their pain and instead of using grief as a springboard from which to launch a new life allows it to paralyse them it's an own goal.

All we can expect from romantic partners is a degree of honesty and the commitment to give the relationship the best shot they can when the going gets tough. It's not for you to punish your father or to allow your mother to control your future relationship with him. She has been dealt a terrible emotional blow but she will recover. You now need to follow your own heart while awaiting the wounds of all concerned to heal.

You are not responsible for your parents' feelings. If you want to visit your father I suggest you explain gently to your mother that despite his flaws he's still your dad. In families when emotional war breaks out it's best to stay neutral. It's the only way you get to see both sides.

I'm Too Young to Settle Down

I'm eighteen and have been with my girlfriend, an actress – who I love very much – for four years. I spend most of my spare time with her, and we have a great time together. I am planning to move out of my parents' house soon and a couple of times we even talked about moving in together (she is living with friends at the moment). My dilemma is that although I feel sure that if I were older I'd want to settle down with her, I don't want to do it right now. I want to travel and she wants to stay here at drama school. I feel too young to be committed to one person but I don't want the 'open relationship' she suggests either. I want to split up with her, but she keeps telling me that we're soulmates, we've been so lucky to find each other and we'd be stupid to throw that away. Although I want to finish it, I value what we have together and really don't want to lose her as a friend.

I don't want to sound cynical but I can assure you there will be many more! Mistakes are like scraps of fertiliser scattered through our lives that encourage us to grow and sprout new leaves. Without them we can't expect to develop. You can spot the stupid people in this world pretty easily and it's not by their exam results. They are those individuals who repeat the same behaviour over and over again, each time expecting a different outcome. It's like the Americans and gun control. Charlton Heston and his band of trigger-happy marksmen insist that every American must maintain the right to bear arms. You never know when those pesky Native Americans are going to break out of the reservations and mount raids on the local shopping mall. In the state of Michigan there are even banks that give you a free shotgun when you open an account.

Yet when the Washington Snipers charge out from the suburban undergrowth, or two teenagers run amok in a local high school, no one feigns more surprise than the people who sold the weapons in the first place. Those who fought for man's right to carry guns scuttle around trying to defend it as an 'isolated' case. How many 'isolated' cases make for an epidemic, Charlton? These are the sort of people who could examine a mistake at point-blank range and still not glean a single lesson from it. What on earth would you want a gun for if you weren't going to use it from time to time? How come kids in this country don't go on Rambo-like sprees through college corridors? Because they don't have guns. Duh! I digress. The only lesson you'll learn from committing homicide is that you are going to spend your life in jail. It's not a mistake I would advise making. There are far better, more life-enhancing mistakes to be made.

At present the only mistake you're making is to keep prolonging the agony. Your girlfriend is behaving in a classic, love-sick, immature way. That's not to say she won't be behaving in exactly the same fashion when she's fifty. Most of us still are. It's the one mistake we repeat ad nauseam: succumbing to the recurring conviction that without this one special individual our lives will not be worth living. Whether we're on our first or our fifth husband or wife, humans have an infinite capacity to forget the love they felt last time around. Watching Elizabeth Taylor get hitched time and time again I used to be awestruck by her optimism. What I've gradually realised is that she doesn't examine her past and decide that despite the evidence to the contrary this time she's going to make it work. She's just got a bad case of divorcee dementia. I've had girlfriends weeping on my shoulder at forty saying they've never felt so low. It's never the right moment to remind them that it's the tenth time in a twenty-year friendship that they've told me that. I'm guilty of it myself. When new love comes knocking we all suffer past passion Alzheimer's.

I don't want to hurt your feelings but I can assure you that your girlfriend will get over it. I hope you don't feel you've made a mistake when you see her impaled on her co-star next time she takes to the stage. I don't think you will. Certainly each loss leaves a tiny enduring scar. Even when the break-up is at our instigation the human ego is so frail that watching another person shed us is hard to do without a twinge of jealousy. Sometimes it takes years to recover, sometimes only a week. The pain of loss is directly tuned to our feelings of self-worth at the time. You sound like you're feeling pretty good. It probably means that your girlfriend will be feeling pretty bad. The balance of power in a relationship is an all too predictable seesaw of strength and weakness. If you're up you can be sure she's down.

As for remaining best friends, it's unlikely in the short-term and perfectly possible in the long-term. It's all down to how patient and kind you are while she's hurting. Be smart (and manipulative). Make her feel that it's really an opportunity for you both to make sure you're right for each other. Tell her you couldn't bear to watch her have other sexual experiences so an open relationship is out of the question. However, if you had a short break perhaps you could both experiment and manage to remain close? Meanwhile don't rub her nose in your newfound independence. Keep your romantic life to yourself. Wait until she's found someone new before you publicly do. Brutal honesty in a break-up is vastly overrated. There are rich rewards to be gleaned from helping your ex recover her pride. The enduring friendship of a woman who loves you can't be undervalued.

Finally, you're just embarking on your 'love life'. To be honest I don't envy you a bit. I heaved a huge sign of relief when my twenties came to an end. You can look forward to pleasure like you've never imagined and pain you'll think you can't endure. Try not to take it all too seriously. Ultimately we're all alone, so no one can 'be' your life. They can only enrich what you already have. And how good that is? Well, that's up to you.

My Fifteen-year Affair

I am in my fifties, and run a successful PR business. I've been with the same man for the past fifteen years, and we really are very much in love. The problem is that he is married. We speak daily and, when I'm with him, he makes me very happy – but of course sooner or later he always goes home to his wife. Sometimes I step back and look at my life and the future seems so bleak. I've tried leaving him but he always begs me to come back. The fact that I've got someone is some comfort I suppose though sometimes when I meet other men I dream of running off with them. I never expected him to choose me over his family and it seems too late to do anything about it now. I'm not content with this situation, but what can I do? It's real love.

It's always real love! I'm always happy to have a living, breathing, salutary example of why infidelity for the

unattached party is like dinner with no food: an empty invitation. So thank you for letting me use you. I fear I'm not the first. You knew from the start that this man would not be leaving his wife. Which begs the question what was in it for you? If you had spent time identifying what you wanted from your life you would have run a mile. Instead you appear grateful that you have someone around occasionally who is nice to you. Why do you sell yourself so short? Don't forget it's easy to be loving and kind in a situation where you have obliterated any form of expectation from the equation.

You talk about how close you and he are. Forgive me, but that's probably what his wife thinks too. A man who has stood back and allowed you to throw away a crucial chunk of your life on a relationship in which you come at best number three in his list of priorities is not the decent man you portray him to be. He's not to blame for your situation but he's certainly been complicit in denying you the chance of a family of your own. In return he's offered you daily phone calls. It's not exactly a fair exchange, is it?

It's time you faced up to the hypocrisy of the situation. Do you think his wife will be grateful that he had secret sex with you for fifteen years? I'm not sure that a lifetime of deceit is preferable to the unquestionable agony of separation sweetened by the possibility of a new life not built on balsa wood. You made the lie of his marriage bearable and have continued to do so for what's fast approaching two decades. No wonder you fantasise about golden futures with other men. Why not try an affair with a sexy *single* stranger? At fifty these days you are merely middle-aged. This is no time to settle for relationship retirement. You've been doing that for long enough.

Your lack of children and the fact you have your own

business are currently advantages. Your lover isn't going anywhere; he's proved that. That doesn't mean you have to stay grounded. Your new life isn't going to appear 'miraculously' on your way to and from work. You have to go out there and create it. Leave him to his unhappy marriage. I wonder how long that will last without you to fill in the gaps? You won't lose him without a fight. After all he's the one with everything to lose. Your sacrifice has made his life bearable; it's time to turn the tables.

Embark on some badness – take a trip, behave disgracefully, find a sociable hobby, seek out new friends. There are plenty of women who for various reasons find themselves in a similar situation. Get out there and meet them. A good friend beats a bad lover any day. Throwing away the rest of your life on someone who offers you nothing but a twilight existence is an act of wilful destruction.

Stop living like a scavenger, surviving on scraps. A partner of your own is not a fantasy, it's what you deserve. He's not going to just turn up at your door as a reward for your patience. First you need to make a bit of space in your life, discard the flotsam. Spring-cleaning doesn't have to be seasonal. Get those Marigolds on and get started.

Should I Have an Office Romance?

Recently there's been a bit of flirtation between myself and a woman at work. Which is great – she's very attractive (she's in her twenties, I'm in my forties) – but I'm wondering if an office romance is such a good idea. A few years ago I had a fling with a woman at work and the furtive snogging in an empty lift etc was great fun while it lasted but very embarrassing when it ended.

Ah, I wondered when the 'office romance' would rear its Serpentine head. It's surely one of the most ridiculous oxymorons in the English canon. Two words that really have no right appearing in the same sentence, let alone lumped together as though they were related. Office – denoting a place of work, where, if you're single, funds are raised to go in pursuit of romance; which conjures an oasis of irresponsible pleasure. Whatever common ground the two can hope to inhabit is mystifying but despite the obvious drawbacks it's a popular sport among Homo sapiens.

I've recently found myself in trouble in the *TLS* (imagine how my heart swelled at the discovery that they even knew my name) for suggesting that desire is what separates us from the animal kingdom. When it comes to the office romance they have a point: it's at moments like this that human desire loses its potential for poetry, and is reduced to mere animal instinct. A dog chases a stick, sniffs another hound's behind and mounts a bitch on heat because instinct tells it too. I can't imagine the same hound tossing and turning in its basket all night dreaming of the cocker spaniel

next door. And so it goes with the office romance – it's the instinctive pursuit of instant gratification seasoned with a twinge of danger.

The office romance is definitely for the Rovers of this world. Mutts who will never distinguish themselves with acts of real bravery and instead make do with the terror of an illicit knee-trembler in the stationery cupboard. It's for people who don't take their work seriously and don't have the guts for a real relationship. In a world where real fear is all too prevalent the rush of being caught with your pants down behind the water cooler only suffices for Mr and Mrs Mediocre. Embracing the terror that someone might embarrass you together in the handicapped loo rates lower than zero in the history of human feats of bravery. It's hardly conquering Everest or hiding Jews from the Nazis or surviving Pinochet's torturers or even standing up to a mugger on the street. Yet the 'office romance' continues to be embarked on and described with swaggering bravado and a sense of entitlement (to admiration). You won't find epic ballads written about it, legends born of it or its ups and downs immortalised on the big screen; unless it's the subplot of a Bridget Jones movie. Nevertheless in some quarters managing to get your leg over in the workplace is still seen as something to boast about.

What we're discussing here is a form of sport, like rugby but with smaller balls. It's got its own rules and guidelines, its own definitions of success and very little to do with what most of us would call a relationship. It exists in a vacuum of covert secrecy. The perfect relationship for the person who doesn't want one. It frequently preys on the weak, offering them the chance of a lifetime, to have sex with an emotional coward masquerading as an alpha male (or female). It's defined by stolen glances, sentences laced with innuendo and an uncontrollable passion that expires at the close of business. That's not to say that people shouldn't meet and date just because they are introduced in the workplace. There's a big difference between meeting someone you like at work and a relationship developing, and embarking on an 'office romance'. The use of that term instantly relegates the relationship to a part-time quickie-in-the-loo, hand-up-her-skirt-by-the-photocopier sort of affair. It's a term reserved for describing a potential series of sexual encounters, not the beginning of a romance.

You mention 'benefits' like snogging in the lift, which suggest the immature desires of an adolescent boy. It's hardly the vocabulary of passion that a man in his forties should be using. On the plus side, as our cities continue to explode vertically instead of horizontally, the world is awash with elevators. If kissing in them gives you such a thrill then maybe you should consider moving to New York or Hong Kong. Or taking a job as a lift attendant in a big hotel. The potential for illicit snogging (of hotel guests) would be enormous and you'd be paid for the very act you so enjoy. Although of course making it public would probably banish the thrill for you.

You appear to be addicted to the covert, secretive and forbidden nature of the situation. If you were married you'd no doubt be having an affair. Maybe you once were? You sound like the sort of man who is having trouble growing up. Aren't you a mite embarrassed that in your forties your sexual fantasies are restricted to the sort of quick fumble and grope that constitutes the sex life of a fourteen-year-old boy? I suspect you mentioned the marked difference in years between you and the current object of your attention because you thought I would disapprove of the age gap. Nothing could be further from the truth. With your immature attitude to relationships you might even want to look for someone a little younger. Even so, you'll be hard pushed to find a partner with whom the eventual break-up is memorable for its lack of complication. Most relationships end in some form of discomfort for the participants although embarrassment is an unusual feature. What on earth did you get up to?

The truth is that even in their early twenties most women are looking for a real man, not a middle-aged teenager wearing long pants and flashing their pay packet. Which I'm afraid is bad news for the office Lothario lurking by the coffee machine.

I'm the Breadwinner, Not My Husband

How can I prevent my husband feeling emasculated? I earn more than him so I pay for pretty much everything – and am *happy* to do so. I've never expected him to have money and therefore would never complain that he doesn't contribute. However, he feels awkward about it. Sometimes I pass him money under the table when we're out for dinner with friends so that he can be seen to pay in public. Other times I pretend I've won things such as holidays so that we can go away without him feeling guilty. Just because he doesn't earn a bean doesn't mean that we should sit at home and both be miserable in order to spare his feelings, does it? We have a full-time nanny too. Would he feel better if he were a househusband? I don't think so, but . . .

What a nice woman you are, paying your husband's insecurities so much attention. And then paying his bills too! You're also pretty smart; obviously all too aware that he would be further mortified knowing that it's an issue. Men, it has to be said, have finally embraced most aspects of equality with good grace, except that of chief breadwinner. The rule seems to be that your salary is a wonderful thing to be celebrated and enjoyed as long as it doesn't exceed his. It's an increasingly difficult balance to strike for a lot of women now that equal pay is not just a slogan. Do you lie back and pretend you're broke? Sit at your secretary's desk whenever he chances by? Secret away your cash for a rainy day knowing you could both do with it now? Pile it up in accounts for your future offspring? Sneak shopping bags into the house and pretend your new sweater is an old one you've just rediscovered? Or come clean and pick up the bill on Valentine's Day while he writhes about in discomfort?

Normally speaking, I'm dead against lying but when it comes to money I'm tempted to make an exception. I can see you fibbing furiously about the holiday you've won; desperate to go and even more desperate not to rub his nose in the fact that you're the one forking out. It's a scenario all too familiar to many working women today and one that I actually think will only improve given time.

We all pretend money's of no account where love is concerned but I've seen some sights in my time, I can tell you. Couples who've been together for fifteen years counting out their individual share of the dinner bill, men with wives flashing gold cards sitting silent in shame, women talking animatedly about their independence while their male companion picks up the bill (again) and gay couples who seem to care not a jot which one of them is paying as long as they don't have to do the dishes!

I hate to generalise but the fact that same-sex couples struggle less with the issue of cash suggests that it really is a hangover from 'Me Tarzan, you Jane' days. Men's obsession with waving the biggest wad looks increasingly like chauvinism's last stand, the death throes of a dying breed. On the other hand for some women accruing wealth smells suspiciously like an act of defiance. It's not an apple that Eve should have been seduced into plucking from the tree but a handful of crisp notes. Original sin is small fry when compared to the problems, insecurities and downright evils that money has the power to conjure up.

Earning more than your man is regarded in some quarters as a vindictive act perpetrated by stiletto-heeled vixens on their unfortunate mate. Not that any blow-dried, face-creamed, yoga-practising, lean-hipped, hatchback-driving new man would admit as much. It pains me to say it but find me a female breadwinner and I'll show you a miserable man. It's not their fault. They've been brought up to think of themselves as utterly worthless unless they are bringing home the bacon. Women may be insecure about their looks but men are insecure about just about everything else. The truth is I think you're doing the best you can in a difficult situation. If your husband wanted to be at home all day with the kids he'd offer. It's not something you should push him towards imagining it will assuage his guilt. Nothing can remove the blot on his conscience that living off a woman has created.

In ten years' time when most of his mates are doing it, however, he'll be seen as a pioneer. If you can't wait that long for him to feel better about himself there's only one thing for it. Go public with your pin code. Then at least you know your relationship will be in good shape even if your bank balance is reduced to tatters.

I'm Furious That She Dumped Me

I met someone at a wedding about six months ago. She shame-lessly made it clear she was easy and at the end of the night we ended up in bed together. Next day I felt sick with disgust but soon afterwards, even though we live at opposite ends of the country, I found myself travelling to see her most weekends. To be honest she wasn't really my type, but she was keen, and it seemed better than sitting in watching telly on my own. Our relationship ended when she confessed to me that she'd met someone else and she wanted to get serious with him. It didn't surprise me as she was obviously desperate for a relationship. I was glad to have the excuse to end it, but I was pissed off that she'd done the dumping – and even now, months on, it makes my blood boil just thinking about it. I just don't understand why it's getting to me so much, given that I didn't even like her in the first place!

Probably because you've got nothing better to do. If trav-elling long distances to see someone you don't even like is preferable to weekends in your own home than you can't have much of a life. There's a tone to your letter that I don't like at all. I'm tempted to have a real go at you. For example, how silly to take the moral high ground about the initial night you spent together. You were as complicit in that late-night-liaison sex as she and there's nothing there to be disgusted about. Indeed, may I compliment you on your choice of occasion? Other people's weddings are all about letting your hair down and behaving badly, partic-ularly if you're alone. For the reluctantly single, watching other people get hitched is like an actor watching a fellow nominee pick up an Oscar. No matter how hard the loser smiles and how heartfelt their post-awards congratulations, what they're really thinking is: Why not me? This ex-lover of yours did what most people do in a moment of emotional weakness; she fell into the arms of the wrong person. After which she obviously thought you were worth closer scrutiny.

It's the anger, contempt and spite littering your letter that worries me. You're furious all right and if it's not at the whole world it's certainly aimed at womankind in general. The trouble is that despite the nasty nature of the sentiments you express I can't help feeling sorry for you. You're suffering a severe dose of self-hatred. No wonder. It doesn't sound like you've got your own house in order at all. You're like a messy scrap merchant peering furiously into his neighbour's immaculate yard where a single crisp packet floats in the breeze. You might be a demon in bed

but it doesn't sound like you've got much to offer on the loving front. You need to sit down and work out why being alone with yourself is the least appealing option. If time off from work sees you scurrying to near strangers miles away then there's definitely something wrong. Home is where the heart heals, not racing up and down a motorway hiding from your own reflection. Your own four walls are as good a canvas as any on which to start conjuring up a better world for yourself.

You hate this poor woman because you don't think you yourself amount to much. In your eyes she must obviously have been 'desperate' to take you on. I suspect you're not as bad as you think. Her view of the relationship is probably that she met a nice guy, decided to give him a shot and in the absence of any emotional bond turned elsewhere in search of affection. What's to hate? If you're not offering what people need you can't blame them for looking elsewhere. Using words like 'easy' about someone who agrees to have sex with you in this day and age marks you out as the antithesis of new man. I'm not suggesting you get all touchy-feely about life, but actually registering your emotions, especially your vulnerability, would be a good start. The world is full of people who are 'desperate' and lonely. You certainly sound like one of them. Perhaps if you stopped wasting your energy judging others harshly for displaying the weakness you despise in yourself you might find time to heal yourself. Get a life, then start looking for a lover.

I Love a Younger Man

I've just moved in with my boyfriend and we're talking about having children together. Which is great – except that there is quite a big age difference between us (I'm thirty-six, he is twenty-five) and I am terrified that in years to come he won't like having an older woman and will leave me for someone younger.

Or maybe you'll leave him for a younger man? Of course he might leave you but so might a wrinkled old pot-bellied prune of sixty-seven. With men you can be sure of one thing. Emotional maturity is one of the most elusive of qualities . . . at all ages! What's important is what you're feeling right now and although it's ridiculously early days I think you have every reason to be hopeful. It's becoming increasingly common to find women going out with men younger than themselves. It used to be a male prerogative, the old codger swapping his wife for an identikit twelve years her junior (known as the John Derek syndrome after the director of eighties blockbuster *Ten* who married a series of completely indistinguishable blonde actresses from Linda Grey to Bo Derek), or the dirty old man personified by Rod Stewart who spends his twilight years chasing young skirt in old clubs.

With women it seems a less tawdry affair. Women don't have delusions of their own attractiveness, for starters. It's rare to find a badly seasoned fifty-year-old making a nuisance of herself at a rave for teenagers. Not so the male of the species. These days the young men seem to do the chasing, and almost more importantly, once they are 'dating', sex, although important, is rarely given as a major factor for their success. I don't like to do a Peter York and start attempting to identify a trend but I think these women are actually on to something.

A hundred years ago it was nigh on impossible for a middle-aged woman to hook up with a younger man. Who would look after them, pay the bills, and provide the lifestyle she wanted to maintain? All too often by their late thirties most women were ensconced in unhappy marriages and changing nappies. Working women have said goodbye to that particular status quo. It's a phenomenon more common post twenties – a notoriously insecure period for women when they're trying to forge careers and establish themselves. No wonder they look to older men to provide guidance and security through this difficult patch. It's like trailing your dad around, only better: you get to have sex too.

But by the time they hit thirty the last thing they want is looking after. Step in the younger guy, full of that burning passion and certainty that is the preserve of these unscarred warriors. They don't know that women are wicked, duplicitous, devious and altogether difficult to deal with. They have grown up with emancipated mothers and want their women out there on an even playing field.

A girlfriend of mine recently returned from Mexico where she met Alex, a Mexican guy seven years her junior. For three weeks they enjoyed a blissful holiday romance and when the time came to leave, her Latin lover begged her to stay. She laughed him off saying she had to get back to work and what on earth would she do if she stayed? He was upset but mainly by her attitude. 'I would look after you,' he declared, 'and then if you want to work I will help you find the right job.'

She was utterly amazed. Not least because Alex lived in

a small house with seven brothers and sisters, most of whom he was helping put through school. 'It was incredible,' she enthused. 'I've been out with plenty of men with money and property and not one of them has ever said he'd look after me. Then along comes gorgeous Alex, without a pot to pee in, and offers me the little he has. If I hadn't been such a coward I might have stayed.'

I think it was probably good sense, not cowardice, that persuaded her to come home, but nevertheless her feelings are not unique.

My Fame Has Lost Its Sparkle

I've become pretty famous worldwide as a result of my job. At first I was absolutely thrilled to be the focus of attention but recently it's lost all its allure. I can't even go to my local Budgen's without being photographed, my friends and family all just want me to do them favours, from supporting their silly charities to lending them money, and I can't think of a single place I can go on holiday without being swamped or bringing a bodyguard. Last year I went to St Tropez and it was an utter nightmare.

Oh my, we are feeling sorry for ourselves, aren't we? So fame didn't turn out to be quite the honeyed cup you'd hoped to sip from. At least that's one area where you don't have to feel alone. As the recently unleashed wide-eyed, macro-brained *Big Brother* contestants are about to discover, fame ain't what it's cracked up to be. Even I in my pond-life position on the celebrity Richter scale need to deal with a degree of annoyances.

At present a newspaper group appear to have a photographer trained on the 200-foot area I wander after visiting the gym twice a week. This budding Don McCullin has so far provided them with two incredible exclusives. Intrepid investigators on 'Dempster's Diary' revealed that I had stumbled into the coffee shop at 9 a.m. wearing Dr Scholls and looking shabby. The nation must have been breathless with excitement.

This was swiftly followed by a whole page devoted to two shockingly explicit shots of Mariella Frostrup 'yawning'!

Yes, OK, I admit it, sometimes I get tired. Though not as tired as people like Liz Hurley or Trinny Woodall must get. People who never leave the house looking anything other than immaculate. That kind of devotion to duty deserves column inches. So I'm a slob, shoot me!

Writing this column is a good reminder of how tragically unnecessary it is for people to feel alone when so many of our problems are shared. Human dilemmas on the whole are pretty predictable: difficult partners, troublesome children, jealous friends, fiendish families, how to cope with death and loss. They're no less painful or debilitating just because they're shared but I must admit it's a rare occasion when I find myself faced with a completely original and unusual dilemma.

Yours, I'm sad to inform you, is as bog-standard as they come. Famous people moan ad nauseam about their terrible lot. I'm not one of the many who believe that it's the guarantee of a gilded life but celebrities do seem to forget that everyone else is struggling too. Nevertheless, you have come to the right place. There are people out there who presume that in achieving a modicum of fame your problems evaporate. Indeed, judging by the hordes of individuals prepared to humiliate themselves on the small screen in a never-ending series of bottom-of-the-barrel reality shows, I'm sure that, if asked to define their career ambition, a large proportion of the population would reply, 'Fame.' Fame used to be the reward for a job well done. Whether it got you a knighthood, a Hollywood mansion or a table at the Ivy, the deal was that you were special. Fame elevated you to a place where few mere mortals breathed the same rarefied air. You became part of a select minority for whom the day-to-day trivia of living was removed by a cordon of employees paid to take care of your every need. All you had to do was make sure that you dressed the part and more importantly acted the part. Your innermost desires and feelings, those emotions and foibles that might remind people you were really just like them, along with your daily ablutions, were to be kept under wraps. You had to be as mysterious and unapproachable as the gods.

That's the part most stars these days seem to have a problem with. You're supposed to maintain your lofty position on Mount Olympus, no matter what the personal cost. Since they started building high-rise apartments to house the burgeoning ranks of supernovas it probably hardly seems worth the bother. Nowadays, fame is common as muck. I bet even on your Budgen's trips you bump into the odd fellow celeb in baseball cap and shades desperately hoping that they look like an anonymous superstar. Wasn't designer sportswear created for the paparazzi version of real life? So J-Lo and Puff and Gerry and Robbie could impress us with how normal they really are while remaining aloof, thanks to the astronomical amount of money they've shelled out for their shell suit. Perhaps I ought to invest in one. Maybe Nigel Dempster will pay?

So you feel put upon by your friends and family. Don't we all? What makes you think you've got so much to offer? Perhaps the reason they only ask you for tangible things like money or endorsements for charities is because you've forgotten how to provide those all-important intangibles like genuine friendship. Do you listen, enquire after their lives, support them emotionally, show you care or indeed spend quality time with your mates? I'm quite sure that alongside asking you to help them out they also ask you for dinner, holidays, drinks and whatever. Without them you're the one whose life would be so much poorer.

You probably think they only want you along because you're famous. If that's the case you're suffering a severe case of post-publicity self-loathing, and instead of moaning about your friends you should be seeking professional help. If they're brand-new buddies who've appeared since you made it, then why is it them and not your old friends you're hanging out with?

Finally, on the holiday front, I really can't sympathise. So many celebs bang on about not being able to escape and then head for the world's glitterati destinations. What did you expect to find in St Tropez? A few old fishermen wearing stripy tops and cycling home on garlic-strung bikes? If you want a bit of peace and quiet go to places where they don't read *Heat* magazine. I recently returned from a fantastic trip to Mozambique, where despite being football mad they don't even know who David Beckham is. Without causing offence I suggest you'll be a stranger to them also.

How about a boot camp in Brazil or a magnificent spa set in the glorious wilderness of Ireland's West Coast, or the most romantic island in the world? There are countless places in this world where people are too busy with their own lives to care who the baseball-cap-wearing stranger in the corner carrying a sureshot is.

Go away and take some of your friends along with you. Fame can be a fabulous opportunity to share your good fortune with the people you love or an albatross around your neck. Your challenge is to make it the former. Check the following websites for low-key adventures for the high-profiled:

www.bodysouladventures.com, www.benguerra.co.za, www.delphiescape.com, www.mnemba.com.

I'm Still In Love with My Teacher

I have had an on-off affair with a married man for about twenty-five years. I'm now in my forties, and married with three children. When we first met, he was my teacher at school and twenty years older than me. We met recently for the first time in a long time, because we wanted to stay in touch as 'friends'. But the inevitable happened and after all this time I really feel we should be together. I know what I'm doing is wrong, but cannot help feeling I should trust my instincts. What do you think?

I'm sure no one is better aware than you, deep down, of the destructive impact this man has had on your life. Here you are twenty-five years later, married and a mother, and still unable to give yourself to someone fully. I'm not saying your husband is definitely the man for you but I am saying your ex-teacher is not. No wonder you are still caught up in an emotional quagmire with this man. Having a relationship with someone that old, in that position, is every teenage girl's dream. It's hopefully as close as you get to intimacy with the man you love most, your dad. Sex with children is discouraged for good reasons and you were a child. At that age a relationship like this is the equivalent of inheriting a second father. No wonder you still have feelings for this man. He took complete advantage of you at a time when you were not old enough to understand the complexity of what was happening to you. He's left a lasting residue of emotional flotsam that you are still blindly, I suspect, trying to deal with. Of course you didn't really mean to marry your husband. You're still mourning an affair you never got a chance to understand, let alone emerge from under the shadow of. You're still looking for that perfect combination of father and lover that every schoolgirl wants but most are lucky enough not to experience.

He's made you casual about the people you should love and needy of the fix he delivers. But what is this emotional craving he fulfils? It's certainly not that of a healthy functioning relationship. If you've read what I've written about long-distance affairs then you're not writing to me seeking approval for this one. It tops the Richter scale on both counts in terms of seismic damage.

I'd like to get my hands on this ex-teacher of yours and wring his neck. How dare he abuse his position of authority and continue to act like a testosterone-driven twelve-year-old. The age gap probably seemed irrelevant because he acted so immaturely. He continues to do so. He has betrayed his family and callously inflicted untold damage on you. I'm amazed you can still find him attractive. Notwithstanding the fact that he's virtually a pensioner, he's probably the biggest emotional weakling you'll ever meet. You are still looking at him through the sunny lenses of your gymslip days. He's probably doing likewise in his hideous paedophile memory. I'm sorry to use the P word but that's what we are talking about here. You are the victim of an abuse you are still confusing with a love affair.

No doubt what I say will make you defensive and protective of your abuser. It's only normal to respond like that but in this instance I beg you to believe me. Put as much distance between yourself and this revolting pervert as possible. He's not a lover, he's an ogre. It's not an affair you need but counselling to recover from this most damaging of liaisons. Of course he won't run away with you. That would mean confronting and admitting to his actions decades ago. You may be choosing to wear blinkers when it comes to his behaviour but I can assure you the rest of the world would not.

Have you ever confessed this to a friend? I suggest that now is the time. You need moral support and I suspect professional help in order to cut these ties that so cruelly bind you to your tormentor. Only when you have addressed and released the anger you must deep down feel towards him will you be liberated from his malignant presence in your thoughts. I can promise you one thing, it will be the best day of your damaged life so far!

You've got so much emotional DIY to be getting on with I recommend you don't waste a moment in getting started. Throw yourself into it with gusto. Then you might finally be free to get on with your own life; wherever that takes you.

Ten Years On and I Can't Forget Her

I have been in love with my sister's best friend for over ten years. It started as a teenage crush, but my feelings have gradually got stronger. We've never dated or even discussed it. I'm hardly her type – her boyfriends are all dashingly handsome and successful whereas I'm a bit of a drifter and I've had problems with drugs. In the past she's been quite cruel to me when I've tried to connect with her. After one brush-off I went away for two years to recover. I keep on the move in my attempts to forget about her but after all these years I still think about her all the time. Should I risk humiliation and tell her how I feel, or should I just try once and for all to forget her? I've been offered a trip through Arabia with friends. Maybe that will do the trick?

Oh for heaven's sake, get a grip of yourself. You've managed for this past ten years to have an angst-ridden love affair with yourself. It's emotional onanism you're suffering from. This poor woman has done little more than breathe the same air and yet you have conjured up a turbulent love story in which she plays a leading role. It's even seasoned with rejections and reunions which appear to have taken place in your mind only. Full marks for creativity, but isn't it time you let someone else in on the act? 'Tried to connect'? What the hell does that mean? Letting your knees touch on the sofa, hanging around her house until it's way past her bedtime? My God, you don't even give the woman an opportunity to express herself. Instead you presume to know what she is thinking, particularly when it comes to you. This 'brush-off', for example, which prompted two years in exile? What did she do, ask you to call back later? If you actually spent two years recovering from a relationship you never had I'd have expected your letter to be addressed from Bedlam.

Knocking yourself down is never a good thing but putting someone else on a pedestal is equally destructive. It occurs to me that by maintaining your fictional affair you've also probably been able to avoid having a proper one. I suspect that any other women you've encountered have taken second place to the love affair going on between your ears. I don't expect a pat on the back for recognising your low self-esteem. You mention drug problems, which of course I congratulate you for overcoming. Such abuse suggests an inability to face the world without a buffer zone. Could it be that this 'relationship' is a hangover from those days? The continuing obsession with a non-relationship a safe way to avoid engaging on any functional level?

You need to glance up from your feet and take a look

at the view. There are plenty of ex-druggies leading happy, fulfilled lives. The difference between you and them is that they have taken the brave step of re-entering the real world. You're just hovering around at the gate hoping a big strong arm will whip out and pull you through. Once upon a time you probably let drugs keep you in isolation; now you're allowing your view of yourself as a hapless ex-addict to do likewise.

It's time you summoned up the guts to approach the object of your affection, but not before you put the relationship into some sort of proportion. Yours is a teenage crush left to fester which has mushroomed into an obsession. This woman may be your perfect partner. Then again she could just be balanced precariously on a pedestal erected for your own private torture. You might as well be having a love affair with a poster of Uma Thurman. I can't help feeling that it's the sort of union you are after. The level of communication would certainly be on a par. The unrequited love affair is the perfect vehicle for the lover who dare not love. Congratulations for being so self-sufficient, but isn't it time you let her have a say?

It might be hard for you to understand but her world doesn't revolve around you. Then again, how could it? You've got more barriers around you than the US Embassy in London. I notice you've even erected a new one by considering this trip to Arabia. It's not the most positive attitude, is it?

Stop running away from life. You won't be the first lover on earth to endure rejection and who knows, it might not be rejection. She may have been waiting all these years for you to be man enough to broach the subject. In which case she deserves a prize for patience. Give her a copy of Yeats' 'Tread Softly', ask her to give you a chance and prepare for an earth landing. Whatever happens it's where you need to take up residence.

How Do I Handle a Nice Guy?

I've just started going out with this really nice guy. He's seems to really like me and wants to be with me as much as possible. I don't know how to respond. Playing games feels silly but I don't want to seem like a pushover.

Going out with someone nice takes a bit of getting used to. We're all programmed to deal with pain but when someone comes along who doesn't treat you badly, doesn't make you feel insecure, loves being with you, is nice to your family and seems to enjoy the weekly supermarket jaunt it's hard to know how to react. If he gives you flowers you think it means he's been unfaithful, if he listens to you too intently you suspect he's a moron, if he calls too often you wonder if he's got any friends. For a guy it's hard work being accepted on face value if you're not a serial philanderer and utter bastard. Women get terribly confused when faced with the antithesis of their expectations. Mr Darcy is our benchmark. At some misguided point in history nice men became equated with a lack of masculinity. The popular consensus is if you meet someone who doesn't act like he's doing you a favour by talking to you he's either homosexual or desperate.

For those like you brave enough to explore the possibility of fraternising with someone who likes you the dating rule book has to be rewritten. All the available advice for bagging a partner is based on the premise that you have to make them want you. This involves treating them mean, holding back, receiving three phone calls before you return one, never being available unless they book you a week in advance, avoiding any conversation that might give a clue to your ambitions for a family, always being in a good mood and a particular favourite for Americans – immaculate grooming. No wonder people get a shock when the veneer finally drops and underneath lurks your normal, common or garden, imperfect, open-hearted human being just looking for love.

I often wonder if self-help books aren't partly responsible for the brevity of many modern relationships. They are full of tips on how to disguise yourself as the perfect partner; which for women broadly speaking means a cross between Britney Spears, Delia Smith and La Ciccolina (for men it's just Brad Pitt). But there's a notable dearth of information on what to do when you're forced to come clean and admit that you're not a virgin, you can't cook and haven't the slightest intention of putting that thing in your mouth. The most recent self-help sensation from across the Atlantic, *Stop Getting Dumped*, suggests a manicure or facial once a week, reapplying lipstick three times a day, baking cinnamon rolls and holding back sexual favours for the first month or two. For putting in that level of effort I'd expect a medal, not a husband. Anyway, what's the point in selling yourself as tuna if the can actually contains sardines?

Confusion arises when someone doesn't need to be manipulated into liking us. We're all so well versed in the language of rejection we just don't know what to do when a person opens up their arms and beckons us in. Perhaps there's room for a self-help book on how not to play games. In my twenties I used to sneer at the notion that mature relationships were less volatile than the series of torturous affairs I was going through. How would I recognise love if it didn't feel like the Monaco Grand Prix was taking place in my stomach? How on earth would I know I liked a guy if I didn't sit at home for three nights in a row in the hope that he would call? Thankfully I've matured since then. More importantly, with the advent of mobile phones you can now go out instead. Then spend the entire evening checking your mobile for messages and missed calls.

It's unfortunate that the only people worth having are deemed the people who don't want us. Lack of self-worth, particularly in women, seems to be endemic. A girlfriend was telling me the other day about her last disastrous affair. It began with a date during which the man of her dreams asked if she wanted a glass of champagne. Sure she replied, and then politely asked if he was having the same. 'Oh no,' retorts lover boy, 'it's not a special occasion for me.' Instead of landing him a left hook she was smitten. Here was Mr Perfect, a man who understood how worthless and stupid and unlovable she really was. This was the man she should be dating. Needless to say it was an unmitigated disaster from which she emerged bitter, depressed and verging on anorexic. The worst thing about going out with the wrong person is who we become in the process. It's easy to spot when it's someone else but while we're being transformed into a grotesque parody of our insecurities we're all too often oblivious.

I remember my happily married best friend telling me during a particularly bleak period that dating didn't have to be like this. That actually there were men out there who might like me, want to be with me and make me feel good about myself. Of course I thought she was insane until he turned up on my doorstep. The truth is that when you finally meet the right person you forget to say no when he asks what you're doing later, you don't care if he calls you fifty times a day, you're thrilled when he buys you flowers, you're touched that he wants to spend every night with you and all the dating rules in the world are rendered redundant.

It sounds like you've found a man who makes you happy. My advice is to wrap your arms around him and don't let go.

My Girlfriend Is HIV-positive

I recently returned to my native Kenya where, after many years of searching, I met the perfect woman. She is sexy, funny, and intellectually we are on the same wavelength – everything I could have hoped for. We had spoken about settling down and I was about to pop the question when she dropped a bombshell: she is HIV-positive. She had been reluctant to tell me because she was afraid I would leave her but needless to say was responsible and did not expose me to any risk of infection.

I still love her and we have now talked about getting married and even adopting a child, but I am worried that it won't work because of her condition. I am at a loss as to what to do and my friends are advising me against having any more to do with her. I can't imagine being happy without her any more . . . Can it possibly work?

Why ever not? I always feel a little gung-ho during the early part of the year. Optimistic for the twelve months ahead and brimful of resolutions to help me improve on the *annus* passed. It usually lasts until the onset of February, the shortest month, which seems wholly at odds with the reality of how tough it is to battle through it. Hope drains into despondency until the daffodils start to bloom again and the Easter Bunny pricks up its ears. Right now I'm still in the grip of New Year optimism and everything is possible, so you may or may not have caught me at the right time.

While you won't be suffering this particular seasonal gloom down there in Africa you seem to be in the process of manufacturing your very own bad forecast. Living with disease is not a choice to be taken lightly but judging by your letter you're giving it the serious thought it deserves. You're also in the enviable position of being able to make an informed choice. Millions of people the world over find themselves ambushed by such killers, whether it's Aids, or cancer in all its invasive manifestations, the sudden shock of heart disease, or one of the many other medical conditions we've yet to invent a cure for. Most people aren't expecting a grim interloper in their relationship and certainly aren't prepared. You have the advantage of knowing your enemy, which makes doing battle so much easier. And there's no denying it will be a battle.

I assume if you have the money to consider adoption you've also got the money for your partner's medication. It makes all the difference. Nowadays those lucky few who can afford the relevant drugs are leading full and happy lives that seemed an impossibility twenty years ago.

It's a cliché, but you could choose a woman in the peak of health and watch her drop down stone dead at the altar. Or marry someone who turns out to be really nasty later

on. We've all met wolves in sheep's clothing before. I don't mean to encourage an epidemic of insecurity, but let's face it, we have no idea what life has in store for us; second-guessing fate is as futile as banking your future on lottery tickets. Unless your number comes up, of course, at which point it makes perfect sense!

A woman I know recently married a man forty years her senior. Her outlook being that the potential for twenty years of happiness far outweighed the benefits of hanging on in the hope of meeting someone else who might live to divorce her. After all, who's to say what will last and what will founder? You've met a person who makes you happy and there's every possibility that she'll continue to do so for a long time to come. How could you now go off and settle for a compromise, having met a woman who isn't?

I'm sure there's someone out there who you've yet to encounter who might make you equally happy but I can guarantee they'll come with problems too. Unlike your present choice they're unlikely to sit you down and draw your attention to them. Instead, as Patrick Marber so astutely observed in his play *Closer*, six months after they've moved in a juggernaut will appear containing all the emotional baggage they forgot to tell you about.

So I guess my advice is go with the devil you know. Life leads us on a merry dance; sometimes a dramatic change in lifestyle or a concerted effort to do things differently brings us what we want but surreptitiously, through the back door. It sounds like your return to Africa has answered your prayers and provided new challenges. Your friends are right to be full of trepidation. They want the clearest route to happiness possible for you and the one you're proposing to embark on is quite obviously strewn with obstacles. That said, with your eyes wide open and your heart in the right place you've got every chance of negotiating that tricky path.

Am I a Lesbian?

I am twenty-three and am, I guess, sexually inexperienced for my age in that I'm a virgin. I've never had a boyfriend; in fact I've never even kissed a man. The thing is, I find myself fantasising about women, and in particular someone at work, who I know is bisexual. She is incredibly striking and beautiful, and while I don't fancy her as such, I often find myself thinking about her and imagining what it would be like to kiss her.

Recently she has been paying me a lot of attention and the other night we nearly kissed at an office drinks do, in secret, of course. If anything did happen how would I ever explain it to my future boyfriend? Some day I imagine I will want to settle down with a man, so maybe I shouldn't let myself have these feelings for her. I feel so confused. What should I do?

You need to let you hair down. I'm not in a position to tell you whether you are a lesbian or not but I'm quite sure you could have a lot of fun finding out. It's also high time you did so. It's easy to imagine in our over-sexualised culture that everyone is at it from the moment they start coming out in spots. It's actually not the case. There are plenty of people who don't have their first sexual experience until they're way past sixteen and quite honestly are probably the richer for it. Puppy love is enough of a torture without having to cope with the complexities of a sexual relationship as well.

I know there are plenty of supporters out there arguing vociferously for the age of consent to be lowered but I'm sceptical about adding my voice to the chorus. Certainly kids are aware of and increasingly indulging in sex before they're anywhere near sixteen, but if I were a parent and my thirteen-year-old was involved on that level I'd certainly want to know about it. To my mind that's what the age of consent allows, a parent's right to protect their child until they're mature enough to do so themselves. That's not to say that the right course of action would be to clamp down on any liaison; instead it offers the concerned adult the right to monitor. There are few situations where we are more vulnerable than in a sexual relationship. For kids the stakes are even higher.

Anyway, back to you. Let's face it, you're not a kid any more. You may be a late starter but you're certainly in the process of finding your own path. All you have to do is keep your brain from interfering and let your instincts do the talking. If you feel like experimenting with a woman you probably ought to take advantage of your recent near-miss snog. You say she is bisexual so she's obviously a woman of experience. What better way to do your training than at the hand of a master?

I suspect that you're emotionally and physically attracted to women while your desire for men is born of your wish for social acceptability. Your unabridged letter mentions a bossy, strong mother but unlike you I don't think your current sexual leanings are the outcome of years of conditioning. Despite all the articles in the *Daily Mail*, I don't believe you can train your daughter to be a lesbian in the same way that you can train her to use the potty. There are strong arguments for nature versus nurture in terms of sexuality that I'm sure you are aware of. Some things really are down to genetics.

I understand your reluctance to discover that your sexuality lies down a more challenging path than the one you've been socially conditioned for. We'd all like to inhabit the middle ground but sadly there just isn't enough room for everyone. I can assure you however that you're nearly over the worst. Once you've ascertained where your libido lies you'll be in the same boat as the rest of us. Eagerly trying to find someone you fit with. My advice is to get out there and start experimenting. You have nothing to lose but your virginity and you're way past the point where it's worth holding on to. I imagine by now it's stopped being something to boast about and started to feel a bit like your old pointy stilettos, seriously out of fashion.

One last point worth addressing is your fear that, should you find a man you're attracted to, he'll be disgusted by your past lesbian tendencies. I can virtually guarantee that there's nothing less likely. Instead you'll find it's a story he wants to hear over and over again. I've yet to meet a guy who didn't fantasise about girl-on-girl sex. You're in a win, win situation on that one. If your Sapphic excursion doesn't work out you can use it to spice up your dreary married sex life in later years. Or write to me again, of course!

I Want to Settle Down

I will be thirty-seven on my next birthday and have been dating a great guy for the last three years. So what's my problem? Well, he works in the oil business and spends long periods abroad. Because he's never here he hasn't got around to buying his own home (he'll be forty in June). He shares a flat with a friend while I own my own. Sometimes I feel our relationship is a long series of hellos, goodbyes and shared holidays.

I'm not complaining because we have a lot of fun and are very much in love but when I try to talk to him about the future he asks me to be patient. I'm starting to wonder what I'm waiting for. I don't want him to give up his job but I would like to see our relationship move forward. Maybe buy a flat together or, dare I say it, get married? I am eager to have children. Am I, as he says, being too serious?

It's time you got serious and I mean about your life. One of the unavoidable truths about equality is that it doesn't exist when it comes to the pressure to procreate. Men for the most part are still proudly displaying their bouncing little sperm sacks way into their dotage. Their brains may go walkabout but cruel evolutionary disparity renders them capable of fathering a child on their deathbed. We, on the other hand, have a finite number of eggs and by our late thirties, like our exterior, they're starting to show signs of wear and tear. For many of us this comes as an unwelcome shock. One minute we're in our twenties popping whatever contraception we can lay our hands on. The next we're approaching forty and praying that we will be one in a lucky minority who can still get pregnant. Most of us know broadly how to make a baby when we're in our early teens but very few of us have any idea what else is going on down there.

A couple of years ago I met a charming Irish couple, both of whom were gynaecologists. They asked me to speak at a seminar on the menopause. My first reaction was a violent impulse to knock them both out; after all, I hadn't even hit forty yet. Once I'd recovered from what I perceived as a gross insult I managed to splutter out, with what dignity and pride I could muster, that I had no idea what the menopause entailed. As I spoke I realised what a pathetic admission it was. Aside from jokes about hot flushes and mood changes I had no idea what the symptoms were, when to expect it and how to recognise it when it arrived. That, they informed me, was the point. I wasn't the only feminist's daughter who didn't know her ovaries from her ovum.

Most women are tragically ill informed about what their bodies are capable of and the nasty surprises they hold in

store. According to my doctor friends the world was crying out for morons like me to stand up and publicly admit that apart from a rough idea of when my period was due my body was my own personal black hole. I could see what they were getting at. By my mid-thirties I'd had three different careers and traversed the globe but I didn't know for sure when I ovulated.

I may have digressed slightly but if you had another thirty years of fertility ahead you wouldn't be particularly worried. The problem is that without the social or religious pressure to settle down and marry and with sex freely available we tend to spend a lot longer making up our minds. This is potentially a good thing if it means that relationships stand a better chance of survival but when it comes to our biological clocks it's beginning to look like a disaster. Your dilemma is shared by almost every single woman over thirty-five and plenty who are already in relationships.

I'm not about to advocate that women set out US-style and employ their business acumen in pursuit of a partner. But we do have to take some responsibility for the decisions we make and the way our lives evolve as a result. In your case there's no point wasting these precious years of your life with a charming, but ultimately commitment-phobic man. I may be judging him unfairly but at forty with no home to call his own and a job that keeps him on the move your man's message is loud and clear. He's not yet focused on ties that bind.

That doesn't mean that you should give up hope but you do have to address the situation. Either you are important enough in his life for him to take your needs into account or he must unselfishly let you get on with finding a man who shares your aspirations. If you spend another three years listening to his pleas for patience you may find that one of the most important choices you can make in your life has been snatched from your hands.

I wonder if all that fun you are having now will be enough to sustain a relationship that's been responsible for such a disappointment. Decide what your priorities are and then don't compromise them. The good news is your future is in no one's hands but your own.

Girlfriendless at Forty

I'm in my late thirties and have never really had a girlfriend. It didn't used to bother me – in fact I was quite glad to have remained unattached. Now I'd like to settle down but I never seem to meet the right person. Instead I take casual sex where I can get it but rarely try to see the person again. I call phone sex lines and have even turned to prostitutes for gratification. Whenever I do meet a woman I think I like I can't seem to communicate with them and end up giving up. Or I have sex with them and don't want to see them again. I have tried seeing a therapist but I lied about almost everything as I felt really self-conscious. Are there other men like me? What's your advice?

Tell you what, you're lucky I'm not single any more or you'd be in for a brutal savaging. I don't want to burst your bubble but guys like you are ten a penny in the dog-eat-dog world of the dating singleton. Indeed there was a time when I thought the male species was entirely made up of men like you. Afraid of intimacy, incapable of commitment, unable to view women as real people, only able to see sex as a conquest and never as an essential part of a blossoming relationship.

You ask me if there are many men in your position: you'd better believe it. Though why that would be of any comfort to you is a trifle disconcerting. You are definitely not unique. There are plenty of men out there, publicly jubilant that they've managed to stay emotionally unattached for so long, but in the privacy of their homes, surfing Internet chat rooms and porn sites while cradling their pot noodles, they wonder why their lives feel empty and lonely.

I'm not tarring you entirely with the same brush. Instead I suspect there's just a light undercoat of that form of dysfunction making it hard to distinguish between you and the truly hopeless cases. You have attempted to seek help, even if after going to all the trouble of seeing a therapist you decided to lie to them. You are not alone in that course of action either. Generally speaking the human desire to be liked far exceeds the human desire to be understood. Hence the reason people spend fortunes in therapy trying to get their shrink on their side.

I had a friend once who used to tie herself up in knots conjuring up interesting things to say to her therapist in order to keep him amused for the full hour and therefore avoiding what she described as 'awful silences'. She wasn't at all impressed with my suggestion that the silences were there to provide time for contemplation. No wonder therapists often get inflated ideas about themselves. All that time in the spotlight is bound to have an effect eventually.

You don't sound like you need answers. It's clear from your letter that you're aware of your shortcomings. Now you just need to stop acting like an idiot in your behaviour towards women. You're a smart guy, you know that the road to fulfilment doesn't lie in prostitutes and phone sex lines, the latter a business designed solely to exploit the hard-of-communicating like you. Your current behaviour is committing you to a lifestyle where intimacy and real emotional contact are both completely absent. I'm sure you're more than aware that this is not the route to happiness or a meaningful (and indeed less costly) sex life. I don't think you're the sort of man who is insensitive or misguided enough to let that happen.

This may be a step too far for you, but have you thought about giving up sex? Don't panic. I don't mean for ever but let's say for six months. So far it doesn't seem to be getting you anywhere you really want to go. You may have a fear of failure but if you're not out for a result then you can't fail, can you?

By backing out of the business of seduction for a while you may find the process of getting to know the opposite sex takes on less onerous proportions. Try communicating without focusing on an end goal and you might actually find you can form relationships (I mean friendly relationships) without failure as an option. It's certainly time for a radical rethink of your approach to womankind. You are being short-changed if all you're using us for is sex. We're perfectly capable of putting on a good show in the sack but we can also be amusing, loving, caring friends. To enjoy those latter delights you often don't even need to take your pants off.

You are deluding yourself if you think you are achieving sexual closeness with strangers. That's just your basic rudimentary sex. Getting to know people really doesn't require that much effort. All it takes is a readjustment of your priorities and a little bit of Dutch courage. I suspect you're in for a pleasant surprise.

I'm Sick of One-night Stands

I seem to be incapable of getting regular sex. I haven't been in a relationship for five years and every time I sleep with a man it just ends up being a one-night stand. What am I doing wrong?

If I had a magic formula I'd be making a mint! You're certainly sending out confusing signals and that's just to me. What must it be like for the men you are meeting? Is it sex on a regular basis you're after, or a relationship? There is a difference, you know. Judging by your letter perhaps you're not sure and therefore not making that clear to your potential partners. I've never been a big fan of the one-night stand. All that embarrassed or drunken (or both) fumbling around seems such a waste of effort with someone you don't even like. 'No, not there,' 'Yes, up here . . .' pretending that they've got a detailed map to your erogenous zones when they don't even know your postcode. That said, I've got girlfriends whose every relationship began as a one-off. Call me Mariella Whitehouse but it just isn't a good basis for anything long-term. If sex was what kept relationships glued together we'd be lucky to be still coupled up after three months, let alone three years.

Sex is something you learn how to do with someone who's worth the effort. Not another form of aerobics to be squeezed in between the gym and your spinning class. If you're going to go for sex first, introductions later, then you've got to be sure you're a really great lover, for starters. I mean most of us get away with our performance because the person beside us really likes us. On a one-night stand you've got one shot at proving you're a bobcat in the sack. So has your partner. That kind of pressure and responsibility can't be good for anyone. It's not like you can roll over afterwards and say, 'Normally I'm really good at that.' Who's going to believe a virtual stranger who didn't have the self-restraint to wait for a date? It's like one minute you're all, 'Let's go back to my place, you sexy beast.' The next you're apologising for having bitten his willie by mistake.

Call me old-fashioned but I think sex is always better with someone you know. The shiver and shudder of the new is over almost as soon as you've kissed and then it's just another name to add to the list. That's not to say that I don't understand your predicament. We've all been single at one time or another and none of us are strangers to that terrible all-consuming craving for the touch of a fellow human being. A girlfriend of mine who'd been single for four months recently popped home to see her mother. On the doorstep her mum gave her a hug, at which point my friend burst into tears, dragged her bemused parent to the sofa and wouldn't let go for thirty minutes.

There are other ways of getting a quick feel without molesting your parents or resorting to sex with strangers. In a decent yoga class you'll usually be treated to an adjustment or two; if you've got a bad back there's always the osteopath; most manicures come with a hand massage these days. Mugging someone will guarantee the arm of the law slung over your shoulder . . . The trick is to grab your pleasures where you can but with minimal emotional wear and tear.

Massage, although expensive, is an excellent substitute. Another friend decided to give up Friday nights out during which she invariably got drunk, snogged (or worse) some ugly stranger who happened to look good under strobe lights and woke up (alone if she was lucky) thirty quid poorer the next morning. A neck injury led her to employ the services of a local masseur. He was handsome, strong, talented and totally professional. She decided to invest her £30 on a nice massage to mark the end of the week, after which she'd head home for a good night's sleep and was able to face Saturday shame-free, legitimately touched up and full of energy.

She started to feel so lively at the weekends that she took up jogging. The man she's about to marry she met in a park at 9 a.m. on her third run. Instead of battling it out with a bunch of fellow femme fatales looking for Mr Right on a sweaty dance floor she escaped the crowd. Proof that the early bird catches the worm.

Sometimes our parents get it right. If something's good it's worth waiting for. From Christmas presents to partners we all need to stop being in such a rush. I used to want to put my fingers around my friend's throats and squeeze tight when I was single and they said I should be patient. I'd still like to inflict terrible tortures on them but that's because nowadays they can afford to be smug. They were right. It sounds specious to say that when finding a man is the last thing on your mind, even the last thing you want, he'll turn up. But it's true. The way to stop expecting people to call is to tell them not to bother. Don't confuse the handsome commitment-phobic moron you meet in a club with the man you want to have babies with. Have sex on your terms, not in the expectation of something else. You don't ask for pork chops in a restaurant and expect spaghetti carbonara to turn up, now do you?

If you can't find an alternative source of satisfaction stop torturing yourself about the one-night stands. Enjoy yourself. Just don't keep expecting Purple Ronnie to miraculously become Prince Charming as the dawn comes up.

He Won't Throw Out His Action Men

My boyfriend and I are moving in together. We don't have children (we're gay), but we are both in our late forties and have amassed a lot of bric-a-brac. I'm doing a big clear-out prior to the move, but he's insisting on keeping his collections of French pornography and Action Men. Is this fair?

You're in luck. The other day I was having a drink with a girlfriend suffering a similar problem. I've been mulling over her dilemma ever since. Her boyfriend's father was a travelling salesman. On his journeys around the UK, he picked up Smurfs from every garage in the country for his beloved son. Unfortunately, the dad died prematurely when her guy was just a teenager, leaving him irrationally attached to this hideous collection of plastic trolls. Now, of course, he won't part with them for sentimental reasons. She's a very chic and successful interior designer, so you can imagine how pleased she is to have them dotted all over the flat. His argument is that these kitsch blue-faced monstrosities are not only worth a fortune – some other lunatic recently sold his collection to Sotheby's for a mint – but also they represent a formative part of his development. He says the Smurfs taught him everything he knows about community and relationships.

The problem I have is that I agree with both of them. Nobody wants a bunch of man-made midgets around the house, but partnerships are all about profit and loss. Many couples expect the beginning of their relationship to mark an emotional Ground Zero. Ideally, everything that came before will be completely wiped out. Any attachment that lays claim to their partner's heart, however trivial, must be eradicated without trace. Into that great big scrapheap of past experience go previous spouses or lovers, the strongest friendships; even relationships with parents must be whittled down to a micro-manageable level. Anyone seen to be too demanding gets vaporised and forgotten as their bright, shiny love train takes off.

In many ways it's understandable. If you've spent a decade dating disastrously, the moment you get it right you're gagging for emotional Alzheimer's. Wrinkles form just thinking about all those nights you've spent downing litres of cheap plonk and bemoaning the fact that there's somebody for everyone but you. 'How come Ivana Trump always has a boyfriend?' I remember one pal crying out in indignant agony. Once you find it, you want to lock that romance in and accidentally on purpose lose the key. The prospect of a night in a bar with a single buddy, pretending for their sake you're only marginally happy, holds no attraction when compared to the all-out triumph of attending a dinner party full of smug couples brandishing your very own partner. In the early stages of a 'mature' romance, gloating is as necessary as peeing, and unless you're an utter sadist you just can't do it with your single mates.

The problem is that it's all too easy to forget how important those friendships and old relationships were in forming us. My friend's boyfriend asserting that the Smurfs taught him everything about community may sound laughable, but he has a point. It's important to remember that without our baggage we may appear to be travelling light, but the reality is we're not all there. Tolerance is the first lesson we all have to learn, if we're hoping for a successful long-term liaison.

Thankfully, Action Man doesn't have feelings so, if he does get ditched, he won't be too traumatised. Close friends, on the other hand, do get hurt, and we would do well to consider their feelings. They're expected to bear the brunt of their pals' emotional ups and downs, provide love and attention and a shoulder to cry on when they're alone, and then put up with being dropped when the perfect partner comes along. The problem is that, although it seems a trifle unfair, it's life. The honeymoon was invented for this very reason. Everyone has a right to fall in love to the exclusion of all else, briefly.

Which brings me back to you and your boyfriend. Perhaps you could persuade him to put the collections into storage until you've settled in. He'll eventually come around to a compromise position, if you treat his illogical attachments with respect. We all have to learn to make room for the emotional foibles of our nearest and dearest. My friends in love are like boomerangs. They fly off into the far distance until I almost lose sight of them, and just when I'm beginning to despair of their eventual return – whoosh, they're back. If we're lucky, it's because they've passed through their necessary honeymoon period – a sojourn specifically invented for those early days of romance – and now want to draw the rest of their loved ones into the cocktail of relationships that forms the modern extended family. When we're unlucky, it's because the relationship failed and they need nursing back to emotional health. It's a dirty job, but it's what friendship is all about.

Which is a very long-winded and roundabout way of saying that what we choose to let go of or cling to is as unpredictable as love itself. So let's talk Action Men, French pornography and Smurfs. They obviously have a hold on our loved ones' hearts. I'm sure both you and my girlfriend could force your partners to part company with their collections, but to what avail? Like best friends and old lovers and demanding parents, there's room for us all. When your partners are ready they'll let something go, but it's not up to you to choose. And if you push too hard, maybe you'll be the one that winds up in that emotional trash can, and not Action Man.

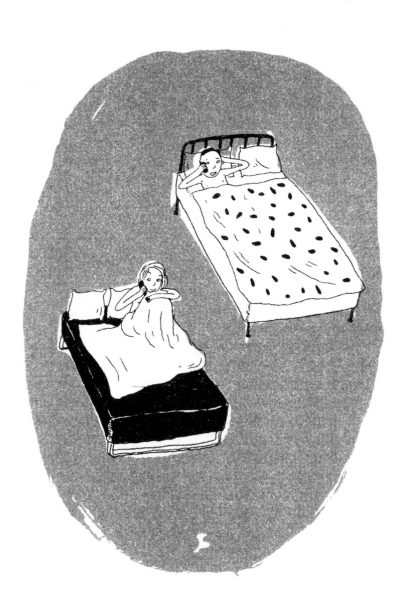

Long-distance Love

I have just become involved in a long-distance love affair. She lives in New York. Can you give me some advice on sustaining it?

Sustaining your relationship won't be a problem, I assure you. Trying to make it evolve into something more is what will present the problem. Long-distance love affairs are hard work. The initial romance of discovering a new person and another city or country is followed swiftly by wear and tear on the participants at a rate faster than on David Beckham's trainers. The exhaustion of commuting, the loneliness of being at once in a relationship and on your own and the misunderstandings that erupt during unsatis-fying telephone calls in the dead of night all take their toll on initially bright-eyed and eager lovers.

We're fools to expect a relationship that revolves around short bursts of intimacy followed by long periods of sepa-ration to give us any indication of what long-term life would be like with the partner in question. Then again perhaps that's not what we're looking for. A long-distance love affair is the equivalent of signing up for a year's worth of dirty weekends. A lot of effort, some passionate inter-ludes and not much to show for it in the end apart from a healthy balance of Air Miles.

That's not to say that it's all bad. It could be argued that a lot of relationships these days are conducted on a long-distance basis. Despite sharing the same home, or merely being separated by a London borough or two, today's working couples exist on such a meagre diet of grabbed moments that they might as well live on separate continents. The combined impact of work pressure, traffic congestion, disintegrating transport systems and general overcrowding in our cities means we have less and less time for those closest to us. Instead we spend our days battling through strangers in a Herculean effort to make a living and keep our feet on the treadmill of twenty-first-century living. It reduces couples to cohabiting will o' the wisps, surviving on a meagre diet of brief phone calls and shadowy bedtime encounters when they finally get home from a long day at work followed by a short session of socialising with friends to wind down. Weekends are spent in recuperation and trying to muster up the will and courage to return to the battlefront on a Monday morning. Nevertheless although this form of existence has much in common with the long-distance love affair it still has slightly more to offer.

Life is all about the day-to-day. The nitty-gritty boring details of living. Even if you're bickering about whose turn it is to make the coffee you're interacting with each other. Long-distance you find yourself just acting! If your lover only gets a half-hour a day with you you're hardly likely to bore on about disputes in the office, the micro-betrayal perpetrated by a close friend, the fact that it took three hours to see your doctor, and so on. Instead you'll keep up a bright, brittle face and try and sift through the morass of daily trials and tribulations to come up with interesting anecdotes and clever observations to keep your listener entertained. This of course is not you: it's a fabulous, fictionalised, warts-removed version. It's a bit like selling yourself off as a supervixen and then just wanting to cuddle up when it comes down to it. It's the reason that long-distance love affairs tend to be fine for as long as they remain long-distance.

If you want to discover a new city without moving there lock, stock and barrel it's the perfect way to go about it. I owe my in-depth knowledge of New York to a long-distance love affair with a workaholic whose arms I would fly into once a month. For my efforts I would be repaid with a Saturday and Sunday comatose on the sofa as he recovered from the pace of living in the Big Apple. Friday and Mondays while he was in the office I would wander the streets of the city dreaming about what life would be like if I moved to the city that never sleeps.

The closest we got to taking the relationship a step forward was once on a long drive back from Boston when after an hour of sullen silence at the wheel he turned and said, 'Don't go back.' At the time I thought he was joking and treated the suggestion as such. I smiled and said dismisively, 'That would be nice,' and he returned to sullen silence. Only years after we split up did he admit that it was his way of asking me to move in. That's the trouble with a long-distance lover. You really don't get to know them at all.

So far I've painted a pretty grim picture but of course there is an upside to everything. Perhaps for you the idea of getting on with your day-to-day life and keeping any romantic business completely isolated is very appealing. *Boxing Helena* brought to life. The geographically separated love affair is frequently the preserve of a commitment-phobe in denial. It means you can carry on with your own life as though you were single while pretending that what you really want is a relationship. So can she! Your only obligation is a daily call and perhaps a couple of flirty emails. Then you can plan sexy reunions and lovely holidays as though you were in a relationship.

If you're a man who likes to compartmentalise it's looking good from every angle. Of course you'll have to develop a talent for phone sex. This is a compulsory component of any long-distance love affair and unless you're a thespian possibly the most humiliating. In your twenties you're prepared to give anything a go and lines picked up from the pages of 'Readers' Wives' trip off the tongue. As you get older the vocabulary of desire, unless you're quoting from the poets, is horribly clumsy. So get used to sounding like you're the understudy for a seventies porn flick, find a phone contract that offers cheap international calls after midnight and start saving Air Miles. Meanwhile keep your eyes peeled for someone a little closer to home, even if it's the stewardess.

I'm Dreading Christmas

I've got a Christmas dilemma with extra spice, I think. Three months ago I met a really great guy and we've been together ever since. I've invited him to spend Christmas with my family as his parents are away on a cruise. The problem is he's a vehement member of the anti-hunting lobby and my parents are country folk who have been involved with the hunt all their lives. On Boxing Day they actually ride past our house! As a youngster I used to ride but nowadays I suppose I'm on the fence when it comes to this issue. I find the killing of the fox a bit bloodthirsty but I believe in people's democratic right to continue the tradition. All I want is a quiet Christmas but I'm afraid to tell my boyfriend about the hunt and afraid to tell my parents about my boyfriend's views. Can you help to restore my Christmas cheer?

I wouldn't like to be in your shoes – or should that be riding boots? Two of the most contrary positions on the current political scene and there you are slap bang in the middle. There's likely to be more blood spilt over your lunch table than in the entire hunting season. Your Christmas Day could make the Boxing Day hunt look as benign as an afternoon at a petting zoo. I hope we won't be turning to the tabloids for details of the massacre. To hunt or not to hunt? Sometimes it really does seem to be the only question. Serious domestic issues barely register on the communal pulse rate, whether it's increasing levels of pollution, the drop in educational standards, a transport system that barely achieves Third-World standards, extortionate rises in community charges, the death of farming.

Further afield people die daily in their thousands whether through hunger, disease or random homicide. Yet in the face of all this death and deprivation the issue that really animates the British and snubs its nose at the commonly held belief that we are a politically apathetic nation is the right to hunt.

You've got more chance of getting Osama Bin Laden drunk and conceiving his love child than of bringing both your parties together in an amicable compromise on the ideology front. Therefore my advice is that you don't even bother to try. There are so many difficulties in finding a partner that frankly one can't afford to make differing politics a deterrent. I don't normally bring up my own life in this column but on this occasion my husband and I are definitely a case in point. We order the *Daily Telegraph* and the *Guardian*, the *Spectator* and the *New Statesman* and most mornings kick off with a ferocious argument about an item on the *Today* programme. Yet when it comes to shopping I'm the fascist. Thankfully there hasn't been an election since we got together but I dread to think how high temperatures will run when the nation next goes to the polls. For all the dissent I wouldn't swap him for Brad Pitt with Bill Gates' fortune. In fact, I can't help thinking that if you keep your arguing (which every relationship needs to release tension) to current affairs you reduce the chances of vicious personal attacks.

Now if your boyfriend is one of those idiotic hotheads who think they can shout and bully people into sharing their position you've got problems. I don't mind entertaining a vegetarian but when they start hurling abuse at the Sunday roast I draw the line. Zealots of any creed are a bore and you certainly don't want to get saddled with one for life. The more likely scenario is that he has strongly held opinions that he would like to argue with intellectually compatible folk. In which case I'm all for it – with the exception of your parents on his first visit. Honesty is the best policy. Love can't flourish without it; it's like trying to cultivate a garden in a drought.

Christmas at its best is about love and family, not presents and dead fowl. If your boyfriend has any intention of becoming a part of your immediate circle he'll have to realise that like a good democracy a happy family is based on compromise. People need to respect, not adopt, each other's viewpoint. Tell both parties what they are in for and then make arguing about it a finable offence. Raised voices a pound, personal insults a fiver. Create a Christmas money pot with the proceeds going to the person who keeps their mouth shut – or indeed to their chosen cause, which would up the stakes, somewhat!!

Most importantly, imagine the sheer tedium of being among a group of people who all agree. That's cult membership, not a family meal. At its best family is a structure based on mutual love, with a communal heart big enough to accommodate who you want as Prime Minister, whether you're a carnivore or a vegan, whether you're pro or anti war, and the fact that you love cats more than human beings. This Christmas put your cards on the table: it's always a winning move.

Should I Send Back My Mail-order Bride?

I ordered a mail-order bride from Russia six months ago. She is nice-looking and all that but she doesn't seem very interested in me. It's hard to communicate with her and she gets lonely when I'm out all day at the bank where I work. Should I send her back?

You're talking to a woman who is addicted to mail order so I totally understand your dilemma. I can while away whole weekends looking in catalogues for things I'll never need and ruminating over what I should buy. My addiction began when I discovered that I could buy Victoria's Secret underwear from America and then use the old catalogues brimful of scantily dressed supermodels as recreational reading for my boyfriend. Being more than a quarter Scottish I love the sniff of a bargain about a 'dual-purpose' item. Within three months I had 'miracle bras' in every hue, a vast selection of matching thongs, a few crippling basques and an almost daily dialogue going with the Customs and Excise men at Heathrow. They had become suspicious of the amount of merchandise flowing from New Jersey to Notting Hill. I'm not sure whether they thought I was running a brothel or an unregistered sex shop. Either way when they suggested they come over and inspect the goods, I decided it was time to return to trusty old Marks and Sparks.

This was followed by a brief flirtation with kitchen utensils. Pots, pans and in particular Tupperware all looked so glamorous arranged in spic-and-span, visually pleasing scenarios of domestic bliss. It wasn't just the equipment I wanted, of course. I wanted the whole lifestyle. Or at least

I had an absurd dream that in my Ready Steady Cook apron, a gift for a one-off humiliating appearance, and surrounded by gleaming silver pans with copper bottoms, I would be transformed into a Domestic Diva. Nigella Lawson with northern (high) lights. This period lasted until my kitchen could no longer contain the plethora of must-have kitchen gadgets, which included a garlic-peeling tube, an inert gas pump for wine bottles, a thirty-piece set of fridge-to-microwave plastic tubs (despite not owning a microwave) and special wine-glass holders on spikes for summer picnics (a thrilling new invention from Australia). I was finally forced to quit when I started handing out gadgets and saucepans as gifts to bewildered friends and family; most of whom only saw the inside of a kitchen when they had lunch at the River Café or Gordon Ramsey at Claridge's.

Mail-order catalogues sell us a dream of an existence. If we just had that outfit, those saucepans, a couple of wicker linen baskets and maybe that lovely stainless-steel loo-roll holder and toilet brush we would feel as smug and happy as the people in the pictures. Our lives would be so enriched. We too could live in a world where the sky is always blue, the windows are spotless and happy children roll around on perfect lawns with immaculate shiny-coated golden retrievers. Unlike magazines the mail-order catalogue places that idyll firmly within our grasp by making it appear affordable (in moderation) and easily accessible. Just pick up the phone and give them a list of your favoured items and three to five days later a lovely parcel will be delivered to your door. Since these days the only other post we receive are household bills, or unsolicited marketing circulars, there's something primal and deeply exciting about receiving a package.

The human brain works in mysterious ways. I am actually capable of convincing myself that it really does contain a mystery gift from a handsome stranger. Even if I ordered it myself two days beforehand. I'm sure I'm not alone. Every day hundreds of happy mail-order addicts rip open parcels like three-year-olds on a birthday bonanza. Even on discovering that it contains those must-have portable digital-bathroom-scale feet pads it takes a moment for your adrenalin to die down. This is because mail order exists in that other wish-fulfilling wonderland, that of the credit card. If you had to stuff handfuls of your hard-earned salary into envelopes in order to receive two thermos mugs that make kitchen-to-car coffee drinking an easy option I think we'd all just get up in time for breakfast.

Now you may wonder why I'm banging on about inanimate goods when you've got a living, breathing Svetlana in your living room to deal with. Perhaps it seems rather crude to equate your gorgeous pneumatic real-life doll with a set of table napkins with bra, thong and apron to match, but that's where you've made a mistake. Svetlana was ordered to complete your arsenal for a picture-perfect lifestyle. You had the job, the house and the hobbies but all those real women with careers and lives of their own probably seemed a little too demanding for you.

It must have been so easy to imagine those cascading golden locks, that perfectly lipsticked smile, and her ever so subtle scent of gratitude around the house. Why, rescuing her probably made you feel like a real man. And I bet you chuckled at how easy it was to liberate your princess from her nasty post-communist life of penury. Just type some digits into your computer, name your card of choice and next thing you know there are Svetlana's flight details up on your computer screen.

How many nights did you lie awake imagining how it would be with a drop-dead-gorgeous insatiable twenty-four-year-old in your bed? When you took her to your local pub she'd wipe the smile off the faces of those idiots. That would show them who the real man was. Their horrible, bossy, cackling wives would be silenced too. The whole community would see you for the vital, sexy, capable, successful guy you really are.

But the reality wasn't like that, was it? Svetlana stepped through the Arrivals gate and she didn't look quite as good as she had in that soft-focus head shot. Maybe she was just tired from the flight? Was it possible that she dyed her hair? Were those stonewashed jeans she was wearing? She seemed grateful enough as she got in the car but when you showed her around the house you couldn't help but feel a slight air of disappointment. Perhaps she couldn't see how great the kitchen would be once she'd got it all organised. After all, it was hard to explain your plans to someone who barely spoke English.

But the weeks and months have passed by and still you and your Baltic bride don't seem to have connected. Could it be because you actually have no connection? She arrived in true mail-order fashion, sight unseen and with no commitment from her buyer. You hadn't had to pound the pavements looking for her, compare her with similar girls, inspect her for quality and workmanship. Seduced by the promise of what she would bring, you also forgot to look at what she would have to leave. She should have been out dancing with boys her own age. Not hanging out with a forty-something bank clerk in the home counties. You presumed she was the desperate one but I guess you now realise that on that level at least you were both pretty equal.

No, you shouldn't send her back. You should do the one thing you seem to have forgotten. Treat her like a human being. She's not a pile of Tupperware or a wicker basket. She's got ideas and ambitions of her own. Ask her what she wants. Perhaps you can love her for who she is; and vice versa. If not, for heaven's sake release her from your grip and let her find someone who can. And next time, how about putting your credit card away and seeing if you're man enough to attract a real woman?

Our Open Relationship Is Dishonest

I believe that true love should open doors and not close you to fun and excitement. I have never been the jealous type and encourage my sexual partners not to think they have to be faithful to me. I am married with two children but my husband and I have always had an open marriage. I only think this works when we are truthful and do not tell lies. The problem is not with my husband but with my lover of five years. He is generous, good company, tender and an ace lover but he lies to me and I can't contest it.

I was looking in his desk for some paper and I happened upon a diary, which he wrote seven years ago. It made fascinating reading and has led me to understand him so much better. One week he had slept with three women: the current girlfriend, an old lover and someone he had met through a personal column. In fact most of the weeks he seemed to be meeting women from this column. Wow!!! However, he unfortunately contracted VD on his three-women week and passed it around to them all. Gosh, what a laugh, I thought.

When we were having a chat later on that night I asked him if he had ever contracted VD. He said no. Later on I asked him if he had ever used a personal column to meet potential dates. Again he said no. Now I am questioning absolutely everything he tells me. Is he lying to me?

Yes, but frankly who cares. I've tried really hard to muster up a shred of sympathy for your situation but sadly it hasn't worked. You think your problem is whether your lover is lying to you. I'm not so sure that's the case. You and he sound perfectly suited. You are both obviously fantasists without a shred of moral fibre. You read the guy's diary, refuse to come clean and then get tangled up in knots because he's lying to you about the contents. Just how do you manage to extract one iota of moral outrage from that form of double duplicity? I'd love to know how you reconcile it in that self-centered mind of yours. 'Wow!!!' you say. 'Wow' what?

Are you impressed that he's so dysfunctional that he cruises the small ads for prey? Does it appeal to your idea of racy behaviour? I know one shouldn't generalise but most people who take out personal ads are either desperately lonely or minority-group members thanks to their sexual proclivities or religion. Being a liar or an ace lover doesn't qualify him in either of those categories. So he's just a person who bottom-feeds on others' misery. 'Gosh, what a laugh,' three lonely women end up with VD. Are you on drugs?

What your letter actually proves is that quantity doesn't equal quality. You seem to be a little naive about relationships, despite having more of them than most of us. You apparently think that along with all that joy and excitement and openness there comes a right to know about every detail of his past. Have you ever heard of the right to privacy? Just because you get your kicks snacking on other people's sex lives doesn't mean you have to be indulged. While we're on the subject, what's with this open-marriage business? I'm not saying that, even with the best will in the world, people don't occasionally stray. But a lover of five years, and a husband, suggests you are having two unsatisfactory relationships instead of concentrating on fixing either. If you're not even prepared to forgo an occasional leg-over in favour of your long-term relationship, how profound is your union? I don't want to come over like the moral majority but really, isn't the world complicated enough without the added dilemma of which man in your life you'll be lying down with tonight?

I may not be answering your question but then you're not asking the right one. This isn't about honesty, it's about control, and it smells to me like you're afraid of losing it. How much easier is it to deal with the terror of sexual rejection when you've given someone permission. Instead of fretting about why your lover doesn't feel the desire to expand on his sexual activities seven years previously why not ask yourself why you're so busy dodging commitment. I don't know if you heard, but 'having it all' was revealed for being the empty slogan that it is quite some time ago.

You are lucky you find the world such a hilarious place, what with girls getting VD and husbands and wives spreading their sexual favours far and wide. Perhaps you're a child of the sixties that has failed to notice that the dream has gone sour? Don't you remember that after the fuzzy warmth of Woodstock came the Ice Storm?

There are single people out there who dream daily of finding someone to settle down with. Who are sick and tired of casual sex replacing commitment and love. Count yourself lucky because you're leading your idea of a dream existence or join the real world where your petty concerns don't count as issues.

Just because you tell someone you've committed murder doesn't make it any less of a crime. It's the same with infidelity. I guarantee you that in the face of all this openness someone is closing up. Your lover is just the tip of the iceberg.

Can I Keep My Old Love Letters?

My girlfriend and I recently moved into a new house. In the process she discovered an old box in which I've kept items of sentimental value, including love letters from old girlfriends and less offensive material like my school reports and my first letter of employment. She used to nag me about my old photographs and once in a fit of temper destroyed a whole box of them. Now she's demanding that I throw away my letters. Am I wrong to want to keep them?

Definitely not. You have every right to your past and anyone who wants you to obliterate it should be examining their own motives. Apart from anything else, wiping out the past is very unfashionable these days. It was all the rage in Stalinist Russia but unless your girlfriend has ambitions as a despotic Communist leader she really ought to look to her behaviour. I seem to recall answering a similar question recently from a man whose lover wanted to keep his Action Man collection. You might laugh but I do actually think the two are related. One minute it's your old letters, the next it's your fridge-magnet collection that has to go.

Getting together with another person shouldn't mean you become half the person you were. To deny you your history is to assert that experience makes no mark on us as human beings. That goes for belongings too. I'm all for pruning. If, like me, you cling on to old tubes of long-hardened Blistex, or one sock, in the firm belief that the other will one day reappear, you do eventually have to take yourself in hand. I'm not saying I have a problem letting go but I've still got the lid of a Tiffany pill box I lost in 1982. The optimist in me is confident the actual box will turn up one day. But enough of inanimate objects, we're talking about our biggest organ here.

In my youth I've certainly been guilty of all-consuming jealousy brought on by a lover's past loving. During my mid teens I became obsessed with a black-and-white photo my boyfriend kept under his bed. I didn't want to admit to snooping but the presence of this picture drove me around the twist. It was a head-and-shoulders shot of a really pretty brunette. I knew instantly that it was the French girl he'd fallen in love with two years before when he'd been on a student exchange in France. To this insecure sixteen-year-old in Dublin she epitomised unattainable glamour. I spent countless lonely hours in his room comparing myself unfavourably to her and obsessing about how much more he'd undoubtedly loved her.

One day I just couldn't take it any more. The well of insecurity, guilt (at my own snooping) and rage finally overflowed. I demanded to know, if he loved me so much, why he kept a picture of his ex under his bed? Two moments later you could have fried humble pie on my scorching face. It was with an expression of pure pity that he informed me it was a picture of Carly Simon, which came as a free gift in her album. The lyrics of her hit 'You're So Vain' suddenly seemed particularly apt!

It's a lovely idea to embark on a relationship with someone with no past. No tricky ex-wives or girlfriends, no children, no irritating in-laws or annoying friends to endure. Instead a lovely white spanking-new canvas on which to project the picture-perfect partner of your dreams. In the cult movie *Stepford Wives* the dream was made celluloid and then turned into a nightmare. Nevertheless it's something to which to a degree we all aspire in our relationships. How often do we qualify our feelings by mentioning a series of qualities and habits we deludedly think we can alter or eradicate over time? Changing someone else is always so much easier than taking ourselves in hand. You can happily devote decades to improving your loved one while you remain as jealous, prickly, selfish, foul-tempered or dysfunctional as you were when you met. As displacement activities go, 'improving' your partner has to be top of the list.

If your girlfriend wants someone with no past perhaps she should try an amnesiac? The truth is that attempting to erase a partner's past or monopolise their memory is merely an exercise in control. The person your girlfriend should be attempting to control at present is herself. I'm sure it will prove enough of a challenge without taking you on as well. Ultimately we're all made up of matter, liquid and memory. None of which we have much sway over.

Memories are something we need to cling to at all costs. Otherwise how do we remember who we are? Sometimes we need triggers to set us off on our journey and I imagine that's what your correspondence and school reports represent. What biography or indeed autobiography would ever be possible without the letters, photos and journals that provide the jigsaw pieces for our life stories? You don't have to be a writer to want to hang on to your life.

One of the cruellest diseases is Alzheimer's, which sneaks up and robs a person of their entire lexicon of experience. From the cradle to the grave with not a single memory to show for it. Stripped of our back-story we're just mammals functioning in the most primal way possible. When people are first introduced, how often do they run through schooling and past friends and current family and old jobs in an effort to find a connection? If you hadn't had past relationships you wouldn't be as fit for the one you're involved in today. The fact that you consider your girl-friend's feelings important enough to write for advice pays tribute to your emotional maturity. We can't possibly hope to be the first person our partners have loved but we can work hard on being the last (offspring excluded). I suggest you tell her to concentrate on making that future a reality rather than futilely trying to wipe out a past that already exists.

He Won't Have Sex with Me

This is a weird one. My boyfriend and I have been dating for almost six months but he won't make love to me. We've known each other since school but only hooked up romantically at Easter. We are both from the same ethnic minority and when we got together I thought: This is it! We've spoken about marriage and everything. Now, although he's happy to go anywhere I ask him and publicly he's very physical, the sex thing is really bothering me. I've tried everything!

Oh dear, 'everything' sounds pretty desperate. You remind me of a friend of mine who found herself in a very similar situation. She bankrupted herself on sexy underwear, tried everything from a fur coat and no knickers to casually leaving porn films around the flat. I'm sad to report that it was all to no avail. He would kiss and cuddle her in public but the minute they were alone he acted like a born-again celibate. At the time we all just presumed he was gay. Nothing else could explain his desire to date my gorgeous girlfriend, enjoy a physical relationship with her in public but never ever take it to its logical conclusion.

It drove her to the brink of insanity and stripped her of all her confidence. Not only did he happily discuss marriage (like your man), but also he spent Sundays perusing the property pages for the ideal house for them to make their home and would endlessly plan amazing trips they would make together. The one thing all these plans had in common was that they were set in the future. A future that never arrived.

He didn't turn out to be gay. Three months after he disappeared from her life (and I mean disappeared – one day he just never called her back and that was it) she heard that he was dating his secretary. Three months after that his secretary was pregnant.

I generally like to take a positive outlook on things in this column. After all there's no point in being negative, is there? Unfortunately in this instance I'm afraid you're in a lose, lose situation. You are dating a classic shag-dodger. This boyfriend of yours is terrified of his feelings for you, or just terrified of feelings in general. And don't get all encouraged because I've said he likes you. With a shag-dodger the more he likes you the less likely he is to have sex with you. Ultimately it boils down to guys who can't cope with the intensity of their feelings, are afraid sex will merely consummate their powerlessness, and therefore avoid it completely.

These guys put sex on a pedestal and leave it there to be worshipped at a safe distance This puts the woman in an impossible situation. You don't want to start begging, you don't want to say that feelings aren't involved in an effort to double bluff them into sex, but you really do want to see if your vertical compatibility is matched horizontally.

It's quite a new phenomenon. In the old days it was all about women avoiding sex prior to a commitment. If men had started doing likewise we'd have come to the end of the line rather swiftly. Nowadays it's a popular punishment at the hands of men who feel they've lost control. These are guys who can only cope with 'love lite'. It's why they so often end up with innocuous, mousy or incompatible women who you'd never have put them together with.

I generally credit it to a terror of emotion, which springs from childhood or a particularly painful early romance. Scratch a little deeper and you'll probably find his parents were at war or his first girlfriend slept with his grandfather.

However, I suggest you don't bother scratching at all. Get out now before this experience does you permanent damage. Don't lose sight of the fact that a relationship between two consenting adults, one of whom wants sex and one of whom doesn't, is not functional at all.

He'll give you a million reasons that initially sound plausible. Take another girlfriend's experience, for example: 'He told me in the space of three months that he couldn't have sex with me because he had a girlfriend in Germany, that he couldn't because although he'd split up from his girlfriend he'd promised not to have sex with anyone for six months, that he couldn't because his feelings for me were too strong, that he couldn't because he had no feelings for me at all and finally that we weren't and wouldn't be dating so why did I keep banging on about sex.' If you're exhausted by the end of that last sentence imagine how she felt after three months.

That particular friend finally snapped, told him to get lost and find someone else's time to waste. At which point he started whingeing on about wanting to be friends. Sensibly she told him she had enough already. A few months later I heard about a situation that eerily echoed my girlfriend's experience. It turned out it was the same guy, torturing another woman. She's now married while he's still single and moaning to anyone who'll listen about how she was his great love and is now his deepest regret. I suspect he hasn't had sex for over a decade and I know of at least five baffled women he's dated and lost along the way.

Shag-dodging is the behaviour of pathological commitment-phobes, and members of strict religious sects. It's not normal, or to be indulged for long periods of time. I suggest that six months is more than enough time in which to discover whether you have a chance of happiness together.

Enough is enough. Chuck him and soon enough you'll meet a man who makes you feel like the sexy, vibrant woman I've no doubt you are! Serial shaggers with commitment problems are awful but even they look appealing alongside the man who has a relationship with you while swearing blind you're imagining it. He'll try to convince you that he's being manly by holding back. It's nonsense.

Real men don't keep their penis under wraps for very long and there are plenty of them out there just waiting for a woman like you. After all, what have you got to lose? If I'm wrong he'll just come barging into your bed to prove it. If I'm right it will be just *after* you meet Mr Right.

It's Platonic but I Can't Admit it

I am happily cohabiting but I have a little secret. I still see an old female friend for drinks and the theatre from time to time. For some reason I have not told my partner that I maintain this relationship. I feel a little guilty but since there's nothing sexual involved surely I'm not hurting anybody?

First of all it's unusual in that you're a man. Most men find one emotionally intimate relationship a problem, two a chore. I've got a male friend who goes completely rigid and tomato red when I start discussing matters of the heart. 'Oh God, you're not going to interrogate me?' he groans and puts his pretty head in his hands! Which only encourages me to do it more often so I can watch him writhe about in pain. Women, more in touch with their feelings and in control of their libidos, are usually the ones who try to maintain such friendships. Single men on the other hand are renowned for their neediness until they find a partner, and then they disappear.

Which makes me wonder why you're so keen on maintaining this friendship? If there's nothing sexual involved then how come you're acting like you're having an affair? I'm all for non-sexual friendships between the sexes but I'm still not convinced that they exist. That's not to say that you should feel guilty if there is a frisson of attraction between you. Admitting to a degree of desire is much healthier that denying its existence. If men and women can't engage with each other without copulating we've come a very short way evolutionarily. As a rule of thumb it's what lies beneath that causes long-term damage to a relationship. You are turning the pursuit of this friendship into a crime against your partner. Yet in this instance it could just be your fantasies causing you to act duplicitously.

I had a letter from a woman who'd been married for twenty years. Before they had their children she'd worked at a law firm. She became close to a man who worked alongside her. They used to go out for drinks after work and occasionally indulge their mutual interest in art with a lunchtime trip to a gallery. As she herself admitted, there was an attraction between them but it was something they chose not to act on. Instead it remained unspoken and probably heightened their enjoyment of each other's company. She wrote because she'd recently received a letter from the gentleman in question, who'd managed to track her down. He said that he had thought of her often during the intervening years but had only recently plucked up the

courage to get in touch. She was in a real dilemma and wanted to know whether or not she should see him.

It was her fear about the possibility of a reunion that struck me. She seemed to think that she was putting her marriage in jeopardy if she accepted his invitation. She could have been right but as it turned out her imagination was playing tricks with her. They had a lovely lunch and now send each other the occasional postcard. It's literary love stories that tend to feature long separations followed by chance meetings where decades of desire are exposed. We all know the scene. His hand brushes hers as they both rush for the bus and two minutes later they're making triplets on the floor of a coach travelling from Aleppo to Damascus. If that sounds silly then how come we believe in the first premise? That two people should suddenly discover that for all the billions of people on this earth their soulmate is the one who used to borrow their library card. There is usually a good reason why friends haven't become lovers.

A girlfriend recently had a reunion with an old pal who she'd always felt represented unfinished business. We spent three weeks working out what she should wear, how she would respond when he begged her to marry him and other important details. The appointed day arrived and she set off for their 7 p.m. meeting. It was a brief encounter. At 7.10 p.m. she called me to say that he was a 'repulsive dirty old man with a permatan' who'd brought his eighteen-year-old DJ girlfriend along so they could 'hang out'. On the plus side it's done wonders for her relationships with other men, who no longer have to live in his shadow.

You hear about dramatic collisions of romantic meteorites a lot less in real life. Nevertheless male–female friendships continue to cause romantic partners some degree of consternation. After all we're only human. Your friendship may be platonic at present but who's to say that in three years' time that will still be the case? Couples I envied in the nineties for their rock-solid marriages are now divorced and fancy-free or cohabiting with each other's best friends.

You'll be surprised to hear that it doesn't mean you shouldn't see your friend. We know that frequently nowadays relationships don't last for ever. The question is what should we be doing about it? Can we remove all temptation from our beloved's path? Ban our partners from seeing anyone from the opposite sex unless it's in a work capacity? Keep tabs on their movements so a half-hour gap in the day is instantly identifiable? Set a ten-minute conversation limit at social functions unless it's with Ann Widdecombe or Arthur Scargill? You'd probably end up not just single again but a candidate for Care in the Community.

You've turned this friendship into a problem by keeping it under wraps. Successful relationships require a watchful eye and a long leash. In an ideal world complete honesty makes life less complicated. If you haven't told your partner because you're afraid she'll put a stop to your meetings then perhaps you're with the wrong person. If you haven't told your partner because you actually enjoy the duplicity then you should grow up. If you haven't told your partner because you're hoping that one day you and your pal will run away together then I suspect that your imagination is making a monkey of you. Go on, clear the air. Admit to your 'illicit dates', tell her you've acted like an idiot and introduce the two women in your life. You'll probably find your theatre dates twice as enjoyable without the burden of guilt . . . and they've probably got some men friends they'd like to introduce you to!

Will Sex with an Ex Stop
Me Finding Someone New?

I've reinstated an old major boyfriend to 'shag-buddy' status and am having a fantastic time, although from past experience I have always ended up wanting more from him and being disappointed. So how can I keep playing with (very exciting) fire and still be open to new relationships?

In short? You can't. The very few women I've met who have been capable of a 'zipless fuck' have been incapable of anything approaching a normal relationship. The fairer sex seem to fall into two categories: the majority who can't have sex without emotional attachment and the minority who can't manage emotional attachment and therefore make do with sex. Men on the other hand have a unique talent for keeping sex and love separate. Apart from Jordan there's not a woman I know whose idea of sexual bliss is having a complete stranger writhe about on her lap for money. Yet lap dancing enjoys enormous popularity with the opposite sex. Maybe it's all part of their 'one thing at a time' mentality. It's infuriating at the best of times and never more so when they're insisting they can have sex with people they don't even fancy, let alone like, for the sake of an orgasm. At what point does that kind of sex become preferable to onanism?

That said, two of my girlfriends are currently using their exes for sex. According to them a return to charted waters is the answer to their prayers. Not only does it keep their sexual quota down between relationships but it also saves hours of re-training in the bedroom. With an ex you can rely on one thing, sex. Removing commitment from the equation seems to do the trick. In a full-time relationship men often only seem capable of delivering one or the other: sex or love. Generally speaking with an ex you can get a tolerable combination of both.

When you're 'going steady' sex is often the hardest thing to come by. Nights spent flinging each other around the bedroom metamorphose into slumped bodies in front of the TV screen. Once breakfasting together becomes a regular occurrence the only spice left in your relationship is in the kitchen cabinet. Out goes swinging from the chandeliers and in comes shopping for them in your nearest department store. New men seem to believe they've done their duty by allowing you to massage their feet while listening to you expand on your view of the news stories of the day. Most of my friends would prefer a couple of hours of horizontal rough and tumble and a Chinese takeaway to follow. This may come as news to the legions of men brought up to believe that we want them to bring home the bacon and save us from spinsterhood. Now that we've taken over the former and relish the latter it's something else that we covet most.

That's not to say that women want sex instead of love. We want both. I lived through the ladettes and listened to women talking brave and loud about using men, while downing copious amounts of alcohol and trying to organise drug drop-offs from their mobile phones. Now the ones who aren't attending AA meetings are married with kids. Look at lovely Zoe Ball – she partied in the major league, as loud and hard as the boys, then married her Fat Boy Slim and gave up work to have a baby. She's back indulging her 'hobby' on radio and returning home to her family in Brighton of an evening. She's never looked happier. The truth is that women don't do very much 'casually' and sex certainly doesn't feature on that list! We're not cut out for emotionless orgasms. For women sex still signals the beginning of a relationship while all too often for men it signals the end.

To some extent I blame the pill; whose inventor should have been canonised by men the world over. The resulting global orgy of indulgence only received a degree of scrutiny with the advent of Aids. By then the marriage between sex and relationships was on the rocks. Men couldn't believe their luck and women couldn't understand why they were so unhappy. It's no coincidence that those glory days of contraception coincided with an era when housewives were popping Valiums like they were aspirin. Things were already way out of hand – early *Cosmo* read like today's *Loaded*, full of instructions on how to achieve the perfect orgasm and then show him the door. Women believed that by aping male behaviour they too could rule the world. We all know what happened. Along came Bridget Jones and all those other chick-lit heroines complaining about male 'fuckwittage' and their inability to commit. A slightly closer look would have told us what we desperately wanted to know. Why were men treating us so badly? Because we were behaving as horribly as them. No man would argue with the fact that women are nicer people. We just forgot it for a couple of decades and decided if we couldn't beat them we would join them.

I don't want to speak too soon but I really believe things are changing for the better. I look around and male–female relationships seem to be enjoying a sort of entente cordiale, which perhaps will evolve into outright friendship. Now that women are no longer afraid to behave like women, men are starting to treat us like women. Which of course is what we wanted in the first place. If I'm starting to confuse you don't worry – I'm back to where we started.

Although your ex may be providing you with a degree of short-term pleasure, in the long-term you'll be paying a high price. It sounds to me like you have an unequal relationship with him, which you've all but admitted is based on you wanting more and him wanting less. This is a textbook route to destroying your own self-confidence and seriously hampering your chances of developing a healthy relationship with someone else. I suggest you ditch the ex, go on a sexual go-slow, and before you know it someone else will come along. Just remember next time that what you're looking for is a committed relationship and that is nothing to be ashamed of.

My Best Mate Resents My Girlfriend

I've thirty-eight and I've finally met a girl who I don't want to escape from. Instead I like spending as much time with her as possible. I've even started cancelling some of my weekend social arrangements with the lads. My best friend goes out with loads of women. He says I'm nuts and that she'll leave me if I carry on being so pathetic. Now I'm worried that I'll lose her and my pal. Help.

I'm so glad you wrote. This column is no place to air my own personal grievances but I'm only human. I've long been of the opinion that men friends are utterly selfish when it comes to their mates falling in love. Where women usually have the generosity of spirit to welcome their pal's happiness, to men a new girlfriend represents a triple whammy of misery. She's female and taken so she's no fun, she's hell-bent on denying them rightful access to their lost playmate and her mere presence is a constant reminder of their own miserable failure in love.

Your letter confirms my worst fears. We've all met them: the rejected, dejected best mate, still single and ricocheting tragically from night-club to bar having a 'good time'. He's the one whose voice blares out from the answer machine on a Saturday night as you and your beau snuggle in for a night in front of the telly. 'Come on, Jeff, it's fantastic down here. All the lads are having a pint, the match starts in twenty minutes and they've got that TV that's as wide as the goalposts. Afterwards we thought we'd go to that late-night bar with the cute waitresses.' It doesn't matter that Jeff is totally happy where he is, or that, up until that moment, his girlfriend was enveloped in the warm certainty that this was where they both wanted to be. What matters is that his selfish pal has sown a seed of doubt and it's growing faster than clematis in the minds of both recipients.

She's a woman so she's feeling guilty. Centuries of indoctrination have convinced us that we are on this planet for one reason only . . . to spoil men's fun. She's thinking: Am I being selfish? He wants to be out there with them. That's why he squeezed my hand even tighter while Freddie was leaving his message. Now he's going to spend all night wishing he was with his pals. 'Why don't you go and meet them for a couple of pints?' she asks disingenuously. 'You could watch the match and then come home.' Yeah right, he's thinking, and you wouldn't mind a bit, I suppose? 'Sorry, love, I'm off to the pub. You've got *Friends* on later so you'll be all right, won't you?'

In fact he's so busy thinking bitterly about what her reaction would be that he's forgotten he didn't want to go in the first place. He's now convinced that he is missing out on what would have been the best night of his life. Nevertheless he doesn't want to start a row. 'Don't be silly,' he replies as he slides off the sofa. 'I'm really happy where I am. Do you fancy a beer?' 'I thought we weren't drinking tonight. See, you do want to go down the pub.' 'No, I don't, I just fancied a lager. Is it such a big deal?' 'You didn't fancy a lager before Fred called, did you?' and so it goes, back and forth, increasingly acrimonious, until they collapse into bed, backs to each other and silent, wondering why they wasted the whole evening bickering.

Well done, Freddie! When he and Jeff eventually speak he'll admit that it was a pretty boring night in the local, half the lads didn't turn up, Chelsea lost and they were home in bed by 11 p.m. It doesn't matter. Fred's call blew a chill wind through the warm August of their relationship. Some people just can't cope with another person's happiness unless they're enjoying the same scenario themselves.

Instead of worrying about jealous friends you should be thanking your lucky stars. So many people never meet the person they actually *want* to be with. They just meet people they *can* spend time with. It's a topic on which I could gorge myself on humble pie. I spent most of my twenties saying condescendingly about certain couples, 'Oh they're joined at the hip,' or spitefully about certain women, 'She doesn't let him out of her sight.' I've come to realise that those are the very couples who are still together. There are myriad reasons.

First and foremost the ratio of saints to sinners in this world is not encouraging. Led to temptation many of us find it hard to resist. Most of us actually need our partners around in order to curb our worst instincts. This is not to say a relationship should be a policed state but a little bit of monitoring doesn't go amiss.

It's also not considered cool to be seen out with your partner. I'm the grateful recipient of the rights of emancipation but ungratefully I blame the feminists. It was they who waved the banner of individualism so hard it knocked a lot of people over. It was one of those early sisterhood edicts like burning your bra. If you insisted on still dating the enemy (men) it would be tolerated so long as you weren't seen socialising with them. Three generations later only silicone can counteract the floppy-breasted results of so much bralessness. Their isolationist stance on the opposite sex was wrong too. Men had been single-sex socialising since time immemorial. Now women weren't even trying to muscle in. No wonder divorce rates soared. What with wife swapping and women's liberation and football

hooliganism in the seventies and eighties couples never actually saw each other.

It makes no sense. If you're contemplating a long-term liaison with someone, joint interests give you a fighting chance of survival. Liking the same club won't help when you're sixty unless it's a bingo club. Look at all those happy lesbian and gay couples. They don't get mocked for spending time together. I've heard that in gay circles it's even OK to be friends with the person you sleep with. No wonder many of their relationships outlive heterosexual marriages.

So let's dispense with all this me man, you woman, I'm off out nonsense. I'm delighted you've found a partner you want to be with. Tell your mate to get a life and then get on with living yours.

I'm Swooningly in Love, but Now What?

I've fallen swooningly in love with a penniless urban-warrior former addict and abuser of most things, forty-two, in and out of depression and resistant to change. He is however kind and sincere, intelligent, sexy, humorous, interesting, beautiful, caring and fun.

I want to look after him and love him when he's eighty. However I vehemently detest urban life, will never return to such madness and live 300 miles away. He says it will take him time to get himself together before deciding whether he can move. My friends tell me that bachelors his age remain bachelors, that I'm blinded by love, have lost my wits and reason. I'm mid-thirties and want a family. Should I listen to my friends or my heart?

Both, because I suspect that they're telling you the same thing. Otherwise you wouldn't have written. Swooningly in love is not good. Neither is madly, blindly, hopelessly, unrequitedly, or obsessively. Deeply is better, and hopefully I've always thought was rather nice. We're adults now. We look silly if we swoon. We know about chemical rushes and the similarities between chocolate and sex, we know about pheromones and co-dependency and deep-rooted neuroses and tapping into childhood feelings of inadequacy and following familiar patterns . . . I could go on and on. That's why we no longer swoon . . . we analyse. I think you were being very honest when you came up with swooningly. I suspect you've got a teenage crush on a man who still hasn't exited his adolescence.

Don't for a second think I don't understand. We've all been in your place before and not just once, I can assure you! You're in an unenviable situation that you will only see with any clarity once your emotional turmoil has subsided. That's no reason to prolong your misery. Maturity may not stop us getting into stupid situations but it can certainly assist us in learning to escape sooner. It sounds like you've made some tough, honest choices in your life. Turning your back on a metropolitan lifestyle for one. Now you are about to abandon that gift of intellectual clarity because you're swooningly in love? You tell me you've met a guy who has to sort himself out before deciding whether he can move. Has to think about moving would be OK; isn't sure if he wants to move would be fine. He said neither. Instead his choice of words indicates that he's piling all his furniture against the door while hinting that one day he might let you come in. Talk about mixed messages! You can't afford to spend the next few years trying to prise that door open.

I don't mean to be the harbinger of forty-something fears. The trouble is I can't help myself. I've watched too many of my friends and colleagues waste the best years of their lives in bad relationships. Your twenties are meant for hanging around with impossible men and then wondering what you saw in them a few months later. In your thirties you don't have time for such emotional indulgences. You have to spot the mouldy fruit pronto and chuck it out of the basket. Otherwise you'll find it contaminates everything else. That's not to say that your situation is hopeless. I've got friends who swore they'd never have children now proudly displaying their third, seen men who swore they'd never get married on their second divorce, watched girl-friends swear they can't live without 'him' and then introduce you to their new immortal beloved six months later.

I hope I don't sound cynical but the one thing I'm certain of is that one way or another you'll come through this. Whether it's because you manage to convince him to follow your path, or because you get sick of dragging him along reluctantly behind you, I can't say. After all, if I was psychic I'd be coining it in doing the lottery show instead.

I don't want to give you false hope but the chances are he will change: a little; eventually. You just sound too smart, self-aware and sure of what you like to go the distance waiting. In your letter you don't mention what you do for a living. Perhaps you're a nurse? If not, why on earth would you want to 'look after him'? He's a grown man, for heaven's sake. If he can't look after himself by now he's at best a slow learner. At worst a big baby. What sort of future are you envisaging? The one you're volunteering yourself for sounds like hell. You'll have to work harder to make up for his penniless state, nurse him through his depressions and all the while he'll be 'resistant to change' and banging on about how much he misses the hustle and bustle of urban life and how he can't hear himself think for the sparrows.

Then there's always the possibility that, despite the moaning, like you he's perfectly happy with his life the way it is. In which case let him get on with it. There's another man out there who shares your ambitions and won't have to be bullied into them. My suggestion is you give yourself, not him, a time limit. Choose a date. Anything from a few months up to a year. Then write down on a piece of paper what you want to have happened by then, but write it in the present tense as though you're living your dream. It might clear your mind and therefore your path. It might make no difference at all. When you hit the deadline if nothing has changed you know what to do.

Meanwhile drop the subject and see how much you've got in common when you're not fretting about the future.

Finally may I just say that I'm a bit worried about this urban-warrior business. Does it mean he marches around central London in camouflage, hijacking buses and fighting for the rights of commuters? Please tell me that he doesn't actually describe himself as an urban warrior. If he does, don't even wait to finish reading my column. Chuck him immediately. If it's your description then I'm almost as concerned. You're obviously trying to glamorise this commitment-phobic metropolitan. Whatever happens, for the sake of the rest of us, keep an eye on him on May Day!

A Valentine Mishap

I have got myself into a difficult situation and I'm not sure what to do. My wife and I have been together for ten years and both of us have a fairly dismissive attitude to Valentine's Day. It seems like just an excuse to get people into shops and florists rather than a real celebration of love.

This year I decided to send the girls in my office, all but one of whom are single, a surprise bunch of flowers each as I knew it would make them smile. The problem is my wife has seen my credit-card bill and she is really upset.

I told her the truth immediately and I've tried to convince her that I am not having an affair but she still seems really hurt and angry. Should I go out and buy her some flowers? I just can't seem to get it right.

You complete idiot. What were you thinking? You can't go making senseless but sweet gestures like that and excluding the most important woman in your life. How difficult would it have been to add an extra bunch to your list? These days loved ones devoting a large proportion of their energies to the workplace is regrettably becoming the norm but you've taken it a step too far! I'm sure your fellow workers were delighted with their Valentine's bounty but how could it have escaped your attention that there was a woman at home who could probably have done with a similar surprise? No wonder she's feeling sore. After ten years it gets easier and easier to take for granted the proximity of a loved one. It also gets all too easy to forget that, no matter how close you are, your partner has feelings, phobias and insecurities that are all her own.

I realise that I won't be thanked for banging on about a once-yearly event that most people are relieved to note won't be back for another eleven months. However I'm a little bit irritated by the epidemic of romantic Eyores who insist on butting their long noses into others' happiness. What's the problem with a having a day set aside for remembering the person you love? We have days devoted to almost everything else, from anti-smoking to poetry. Bravo for a day devoted to going all out and saying I love you, loud and clear, once a year. If I were Prime Minister I'd make it a bank holiday.

Dissenters like you frequently go for the anti-consumerist tack. Spare me. No one is going to put a gun to your head and force you to dial Interflora, or indeed frogmarch you into one of the many card shops on the high street boasting an exhaustive display of saccharine messages for all seasons. You can exercise your free will on Valentine's Day as much as you can on any other but that's no excuse not to exercise your imagination.

The Valentine I remember most fondly was a handmade card, with the words of 'These Foolish Things' written in gold ink and decorated with musical notes and little illustrations in the margins. I still to this day don't know who the sender was. They obviously couldn't care less about being identified, had spent time and effort on their creation, and expected no reward at all. Not even recognition. If that's not the definition of love then I don't know what is. Their pleasure was, quite literally, my pleasure. Although this happened sixteen years ago the memory of that selfless gesture still cheers me up and intrigues me today.

For romance assassins the other argument against a day devoted to lovers is that love should be celebrated all year round. Again, spare me the lecture. How many people do actually remember to make those little all-important gestures as often as they'd like to, or like to think they do? Pick up a posy on the way home, buy a book they know their partner will love, cook a surprise meal when their spouse is tired and emotional.

The biggest threat to relationships is not infidelity but carelessness. Most of the relationship-breakdown letters I receive aren't from those whose partners have cheated on them sexually but from lonely people whose partners have forgotten to love them properly. I'm not trying to build K2 out of a mere molehill here but maybe your wife's hurt and anger isn't solely inspired by this latest example of thoughtlessness towards her. Could it be that examined closer you might register an accruing of neglect that's finally starting to take its toll?

I believe that you aren't having an affair and I suspect your wife does too. That doesn't mean she has cause for celebration. I'm suspicious of your motives for sending this floral round robin to your female staff. Was there perhaps a particular person you felt most sympathetic to but being a decent married man wouldn't have dreamt of singling out for attention? Perhaps it was just the vaguest surprise whiff of romance past that got you feeling all sentimental? Whatever the case you need to look sharp and start thinking about what's important in your life.

With ten years of marriage under your belt this is no time to get careless. How about spreading a little of that bountiful largesse of yours where it counts? Don't try to freshen up the décor at home merely by making yourself a nuisance at your local flower shop. Instead start thinking of your wife as a separate human being and rising to the challenge of bringing a smile of surprise and joy to her face. Maybe she'd like a new CD, maybe she'd like you to tidy the attic or maybe she'd like to go out and get drunk with you.

Showing kindness to strangers is the easy option. Showing kindness to those you love is an altogether more satisfying and neglected art.

Feminism Destroyed My Marriage

I recently separated from my wife who decided she wanted independence and a chance to lead her own life. For a long time she'd sat silent, quietly soaking up the feminist doctrines being spouted from every corner of the media, and never raising her voice in defence of men. I think it eventually went to her head. I know she'll regret it and ask me to return but, after suffering nearly twenty years with her, and bringing up four daughters, I now find female company unbearable. I blame feminism entirely. Is this wrong?

You poor wounded creature. Only the most hard-hearted of She-Devils could read your letter without feeling a sliver of remorse. That you should have been so victimised by a rabid minority sect with nothing better to do than fight for sexual parity is an outrage. You, my dear fellow, have been abused. Years and years of being ground down, whittled into a mere sliver of your former macho self by these hideous vengeful Furies. No wonder you said enough is enough. How could your wife have just sat there, head down, eyes glued to her knitting, and not spoken up for you when her fellow sex were 'gushing' forth on men's foibles. Anyone would think she was afraid to speak her mind. Not a state that you could be held in any way responsible for, I'm sure.

What kind of woman could listen to those sexist sermons, watch women roughing up men at every opportunity, condone her sisters' duplicitous behaviour, be that insensitive to her partner's needs and then expect her marriage to carry on as normal? It defies belief. She was looking for a saint and not a husband. As you say, she'll regret it. No woman is happier than with husband and child, particularly if she can stay at home and look after the baby while her man goes out and braves the big wide world on her behalf.

It's not that I don't think men get a hard time. Just the other night I was out at dinner with a couple of girlfriends who seemed to thinks guys were the funniest creatures on the planet. They were cackling like banshees as they related their stories. 'So he says to me, "You'd look good in my Golf." I told him he was confusing a relationship with accessorising.' 'You think that's bad? Do you remember that guy who ran a mile every time I started liking him? He turned up at the flat on Saturday, said he'd made a mistake, started kissing me and then jumped up and left yelling something about how he was double-parked. He can't even commit to a parking space, for Christsakes!'

As I listened I did start to feel a little guilty. If I overheard two guys in a pub speaking with equal vehemence about women I'd probably have to challenge them. The law and the landlord would be on my side. Yet if we'd been interrupted by a pair of well-meaning men who felt we were going too far we'd have given them at best a good tongue-lashing followed by a humourless history lesson. After all, we've got centuries of injustice providing fodder for our fury.

These days I admit we do occasionally abuse it. We're like bullies who've discovered their power and just can't stop reminding their victims who's boss. But you guys are such easy targets, it's like shooting a duck that's handcuffed to your bedpost. Quack . . . splat . . . hardly sport at all.

Twenty-first-century men and women behave like long-married couples who keep the spice in their relationship by maintaining a constant verbal battle. To the untrained ear it sounds like discord but to the people who know them it's obvious they're just playing. We've got so used to teasing and taunting each other we've forgotten that some people take us seriously. Perhaps you've taken things a little too literally? Extremes of opinion are all the rage in a media-led world. You've been so busy being beaten by the rhetoric that you've forgotten to look around and see how things balanced out in reality.

Lighten up a little, why don't you? I suspect your wife didn't defend you against the feminist onslaught because she was too busy bringing up four daughters. I don't think you can blame her for your sense of victimisation at the hands of hideous mouthy crones like me. Perhaps you should try being friends. She and your daughters could provide an excellent buffer zone between you and the sisterhood. Without them you'll be mauled to death in moments if you open your mouth.

Truly, I'm forced to dab my way through a box of man-sized Kleenex when I think about how terrible the world must be for men like you. My tears pour like a fountain of grief, carrying a tsunami of guilt at the injustices perpetrated since those nasty feminists got going. When you leave home in the morning, even in the remotest corners of the world, you can no longer look forward to a blissful eight hours *femme*-free. Instead the minute you shut the front door on your family you're faced with a barrage of women outside. Waving parking tickets at you, trying to arrest you, cutting you up on the motorway, telling you you're sacked, beaming from your TV screen, blaring from your radio, sorting out your plumbing. No wonder you seek refuge in your own company. Anything must be preferable to engaging with those ghastly women who seem to have taken over the world.